GHOSTS
of Gettysburg
III

*Spirits, Apparitions and Haunted
Places of the Battlefield*

by
Mark Nesbitt

THOMAS PUBLICATIONS
Gettysburg PA 17325

To Barbara

Who always believed

Welcome peaceful bed
When our camps expire.
Though no tears be shed,
Though no tuneful choir
Chant in mournful strains
While around our bier:
Yet a rest remains
Long denied us, here.

— Lexington Presbyterian Cemetery
(burial site of "Stonewall" Jackson)
in Lexington, Virginia

No more the bugle calls the weary one
Rest, noble spirit in the grave unknown,
We will find you, we will know you
Among the good and true
When the robe of white is given
For the faded coat of blue.

— Monument to Union soldiers in Kipton, Ohio

CONTENTS

ACKNOWLEDGEMENTS

Once again, I am forced, as all writers are sooner or later, to admit that I have had a great deal of help creating this work. Many individuals are involved in the research, writing, and publication of a book, and without the assistance of the following people, this one could never have been written.

I must acknowledge Dean and Jeane Thomas of Thomas Publications in Gettysburg. Be aware that the "professional" historians are not the only ones coming out with good, solid historical works; there are people who have researched a topic for a lifetime and are creating terrific books about the Civil War and Gettysburg. Dean and Jeane are publishing these experts, who, for various reasons, may never win a Pulitzer Prize, but are, nevertheless, the best in their field. Thanks also go out to Marguerite Plank, my editor at Thomas Publications.

I must also acknowledge fellow historian and author Gregory Coco for his dedicated research on the Campaign and Battle of Gettysburg. No matter what book I've been working on, he seems to come up with a pertinent historical fact from his files that adds to the story.

Dr. Walter Powell, author and preservation officer of the Borough of Gettysburg, and Elwood "Woody" Christ have also been there when I needed access to their research at the borough building.

Steve Wolf, Denise Clark, and Deb Hagen at the Herr Tavern and Publick House were always helpful no matter how busy their schedules.

I owe a thank-you to Lynn Goddard for missing her in my last book. My long-time friend Goretti Schrade and Rebecca Krishan added a story to this collection, as did Mary Sutphen of the American Print Gallery in Gettysburg and Susan Sutphen of Gettysburg One-Hour Photo.

Joe and Colette Hood graciously opened their home to me, as did Mark and Diana Snell. Pam Saylor, a gifted psychic, in a speech and in subsequent discussions, gave me additional insight into the paranormal world. Dane Wagle and Mr. and Mrs. F. William Wagle shared with me one of the unexplainable events that happened to them.

This wouldn't be one of my ghost books without the help of my friends Karyol Kirkpatrick and Dr. Charles Emmons who both generously shared their vast knowledge and experiences in the field of parapsychology.

Erica and Tom Crist, Jennifer Musumeci, Eric Persson, and Steve Hammond all contributed their strange experiences in Gettysburg. Eric Johnson contacted me from California to relate the incredible number of mysterious happenings during the filming of the movie "Gettysburg."

Bob and Georgia Servant and Kevin Servant of Servant's Old Tyme Photos in Gettysburg allowed me access to research one of the stories. Diane Brennan at the Wills House, shared her experiences as well.

Darla Peightal and Jennifer Suroviec were kind enough—and courageous enough—to share a story that allowed a legend to become a documentable fact. Glenn Sitterly shared his knowledge, and Priscilla R. Baker, fellow author, helped with one of the stories.

To those I have spoken with and who have encouraged me in this work, yet haven't been mentioned in these acknowledgments, I apologize and say a heartfelt thanks.

INTRODUCTION

The invisible, ethereal soul of man resisting and overcoming the material forces of nature; scorning the inductions of logic, reason, and experience. persisting in its purpose and identity; this elusive apparition between two worlds unknown, deemed by some to be but the chance product of intersecting vortices of atoms and denied to be even a force...
                                        —Maj. Gen. Joshua L. Chamberlain

They come at night often. And often they come into your most private, intimate time: sleep. It is as if unconsciousness—like madness—is some sort of inroad to where they live and play. But they also show themselves in broad daylight, making their appearance even more mysterious by *not* being so mysterious as to use darkness for a cover.

They manifest themselves in many guises, using all your senses. Auditory apparitions seem to be the most common, accounting for about 60 percent of the experiences; but all the senses are involved, including that unnamed sense that simply tells you something is not quite right by sending that special chill.

And they manifest themselves just about anywhere—at the foot of your bed, across a sun-showered field, through a window or door, or sometimes as just light or shadow. But, we know, they especially show themselves at Gettysburg.

"They," of course, are "ghosts." "Spirits" may be a better, less volatile term, but we're talking about the same thing. A sound, a smell, of something that is long gone; a vision, a touch out of time and beyond reason, of someone who is dead.

And perhaps "dead" isn't the right word either, with its connotations of finality and eventual decay. If the spirit is the very essence of the person, and the body is something it just lives in and breathes out of for a while, then maybe the word for the moment of cessation of the living body in terms of what the spirit does is "to move on."

Some people even think that these apparitions are demons sent to confuse us. If they are, they're pretty impotent demons, for only rarely do you ever hear of an apparition harming anyone physically. In fact, of all the stories of ghosts I've collected, none has ever harmed a living human being.

So, it seems that in virtually all the cases, all "they" want is to be noticed. And this is very sad.

When I first embarked upon collecting, relating, and documenting the ghost stories of Gettysburg, Col. Jacob M. Sheads, the renowned Gettysburg historian, suggested that I might be opening up a Pandora's box about the battlefield. Again, as one who has been here long enough to know, he was right.

But his allegory fell a little short. The Pandora's box that was opened contained not just unanswerable questions about the Gettysburg battlefield. Emerging unbidden from that mythical box were questions about life and death, heaven and hell, time and energy, existence and the eternities. What also has emerged is the absolute assurance that there are far more things in this world that we don't understand than those we do.

Mysteries are inherent in all of life. Perhaps that's all that life is. The questions may sound trite, but they *are* important: why are we here? Is there a purpose to it all? Is what we see around us real; or is *this* the illusion and whatever comes after the reality?

There are the eternal questions: What happens to the dead, or to us when we die? Is the cessation of movement reality or just an illusion as it is in the autumn when trees and flowers seem to die, but don't really? Is this life just a preparation for the next?

Why should we be so reluctant to admit that there are mysteries about paranormal activities? Are we humans such egotists that we think we should or will be able to explain everything in this incredible, fabulous, unexplainable world?

Why do spirits linger at a place of emotional turmoil? Is a violent, horrible, unexpected death the criteria for remaining behind, for, if you will, life after death?

Who's to say, if time is not linear, that we may be able to "circle back around," and be reincarnated into the past?

Or that if reincarnation does occur, and we have already been reincarnated, that when we see a ghost, we might be looking at our own previous incarnation, looking at our own self as we were in the past?

And though it seems that death instigates all these questions, it is more likely that it is death which answers them all.

There have been other, more personal questions, to me, as well. Have I ever seen a ghost? That I can only answer by saying, "I think so." I have only had five experiences that I cannot explain while living in Gettysburg. One of the five was visual; one was olfactory; the rest were auditory; and there were the "feelings" I got in certain houses and on certain parts of the battlefield that told me I should not be there at that time.

Do I believe in ghosts? I respond to that with two answers. First, I know that humans are not at the end-point of their knowledge, that someday we will discover just what kind of energy it is that produces apparitions. Second, I believe, like billions of others on this planet, that something goes on after death; that death is not a closing door, but one that is opening.

Are these stories true? I can assure people that I did not fabricate a single one. (Although many times, as a writer, I have wished I had that immense amount of

vity!) All the stories I have included in the three books have been told to
or the most part, by the people who have experienced them. Some were
reluctant to tell them for they were frightened so badly by the experience that it
was painful to recount. Some cried when they told their story; others got that
certain chill and gooseflesh while telling their stories. Whether I believe in ghosts
or not is immaterial; I do believe the people who have told me their stories. I am
convinced that what they said happened *really* happened.

Some of their experiences occurred before the witnesses even knew of my two
previous ghost books. Some stories, such as sightings of the "Woman in White,"
have just recently surfaced from notes Dr. Charles Emmons took while inter-
viewing people ten years before *Ghosts of Gettysburg* was ever printed.

Unexplainable events continue to happen out on the battlefield, in both new
places and some places that have been documented before. So some of these
stories are "updates" on stories from the previous books. Some are revisitations
of sites that appear to be permanently haunted that were included in the other
books. Some of the stories in this book involve sites that I'd always heard had
strange, ghostly happenings but that I did not have a chance to include in the last
books.

I think people feel comforted by the thought that there may be something that
goes on after we die. No doubt, for some people, there is a spirit connection of
the heart that grows from love and goes beyond life and into the other world, as
when people go to gravesites and talk to loved ones gone before them. Ask anyone who has done it: There is a full, enriching communication, an unburdening
of the heart.

Perhaps the place we have named Gettysburg, where at least one great battle
was fought, can be thought of as a cauldron, a refiner's fire, where, while some
lives were ended, others were created whose tendrils somehow reach across the
ages to us. Perhaps we are forever connected with that "spirit connection" to
them. What Maj. Gen. Joshua L. Chamberlain wrote of the soldiers who fought
and sacrificed during the war could apply to us as well: "They belonged to me,
and I to them, by bonds birth cannot create nor death sever."

THE PREMATURE BURIAL

The boundaries which divide Life from Death,
are at best shadowy and vague.
Who shall say where one ends,
and where the other begins?

—Edgar Allen Poe

There can be no horror more acute, more unthinkable, than that of being buried alive.

Awakening in the dark, your last memory is of your loving family gathered around your bedside. You think your eyes are open, but you cannot be sure, so you lift your hands to turn on the light and they suddenly thump into the satin-lined lid, just inches from your chest. You squeeze your arms between your body and the lid. A panicky tactile search in front of your face, and you touch the satin again just a claustrophobic inch or two from your nose. You lift your body to sit up and your forehead bangs into the coffin lid, and your arms cannot get leverage to push the lid open with tons of earth above. You try and turn on your side to get more leverage, but there is no turning in the form-fitted, eternal reclining-place. Your shoulder, your forearms, your head against the lid, and a push with whatever feeble effort you can muster does no good; the soft satin gives but the lid is locked tight. You scream into the fabric and hurt your own ears...but no one hears. Panic rises with the realization of where you are, that you can barely move and worse—that no one knows, and the only thing you can think of is, how long...how long...how long will I have to wait in the dark before I die?

Some say that in the old days, when churches were moved and their graveyards dug up, occasionally an opened coffin would reveal a shrivelled, dried-up corpse with its fingernails dug into the ancient cloth lining of the casket and the leathery jaw tight against the breast in a scream that was never heard. That is why, when people were thought to have died, a mirror was called for and held under their noses. Even the slightest fog on the surface would indicate life and burial would be postponed, for it is most horrible when an interment is premature.

Apparently, after the Battle of Gettysburg, there was such an accidental, inescapable incarceration of one thought dead, but under even more horrible circumstances.

The first day's fighting of the three-day battle was over. It had swirled across the farm fields to the west, north and east of the Pennsylvania crossroads town.

Over the ridge named for the Lutheran Theological Seminary it crested, then down into the town itself, leaving the ridge to the commander of the Southern forces, Gen. Robert E. Lee.

Of course, all about the area was the human refuse of battle: corpses and pieces of corpses, flung like some mad butcher was at work, as indeed Death was that hot first day of July. Perhaps it was because the commanding general was so near that the clean-up crews were in such a hurry to remove the hideous relics of combat. Some burials were going on in the distance, no doubt, but in the vicinity of Lee's headquarters, it is likely his aides directed the burial crews to expedite their work.

Often, ice houses, or cool corners of cellars were used to temporarily store bodies until the burial crews could come around and pick them up.[1] That is probably what happened in this case, although with an awful twist.

Like cordwood, the human remains were rapidly stacked in the small stone room below Mrs. Thompson's wooden barn across the Chambersburg Road from her tidy stone house, piled there quickly out of the hot sun and from the commander's view for the next three and a half days, while the battle raged on other fronts. Not that it mattered at all to the cold, stiffening corpses in the little stone room. Except that it did matter to one of those piled there....

The battle was over and the Confederates had begun their retreat westward to the mountains. Slowly, cautiously, the Union skirmishers pressed out the Chambersburg Road. It was probably dreary, miserable and raining—since that was the weather generally in the days following the battle—when someone opened the door on the lower floor of the Thompson's barn and discovered the gruesome mound of humanity, now putrefying in the small back room.

One by one they began to pull the bloated, stiff bodies off the pile and carry them out for burial. Slowly the horrid hill began to dissolve. As they grabbed the arms and legs of one of the bodies that had been trapped on the bottom of the disgusting stack, suddenly one of its hands convulsed. The "dead" eyelids flew open and the eyes stared, then circled in a madman's panicked gaze. The startled burial party dropped its writhing bundle unceremoniously back onto the pile.

For four days he had lain, buried alive under that festering mound of dead men, paralyzed himself by his wound and unable to crawl out. When he did regain consciousness, he found himself under hundreds of pounds of decaying human flesh and bone thrown on top of him. Lying there, with only the dead for company, wondering if he would ever be found, he must have felt very much buried alive, only not in some comfortable, satin-lined coffin, but in a more awful sarcophagus. They say when they brought him out into the fresh air, he was raving. He himself joined the dead just a few days later and was buried properly this time.

But something of his essence apparently has not altogether left the stone-walled room where he lay buried alive. Some horrified piece of his soul seemingly remains, still pushing in vain against the coffin-lid of human flesh that had entombed him.

Field of Lee's headquarters and the Thompson barn site

Though the Thompson barn burned and a modern dwelling was built over it, the small stone room remained as part of the basement. It had been closed off by a door and contained nothing of importance to the infrastructure of the house— no pipes or ducts or wires and still had the ancient earth floor which had absorbed the juices of the decaying soldiers once placed there for storage.

Like all houses, this one had its own indigenous moans and groans, its creakings and tappings to which all owners become accustomed. But some occupants recently reported an otherworldly cacophony that defied all logical explanation and seemed to emanate only from the stone room in the basement once used as a makeshift mausoleum.

It began late one quiet summer night. The family was sound asleep. Suddenly, from within the bowels of the house came an unearthly, incredible roar as if someone had placed a bomb in the furnace. One occupant of the house, crawling bravely from the safety of bed, tried to pass through the kitchen to the cellar, only to realize that everything there was moving. Cups and glasses in the cupboards rattled and fell; toasters and can openers and breadboxes slid about on the sinkboards; and in the hall, pieces of furniture were being propelled from one wall to the other by some unseen force.

Descending into the darkened cellar, the occupant, now joined by another, realized that the noises were growing into a steady, heavy pounding, coming from back in the corner. Approaching the rear corner of the cellar confirmed the worst nightmare: the door to the small stone room was the source of the rhythmic, desperate hammering and the door itself was heaving with the blows heavily against its own hinges.

They fled the basement and realized that there was only one thing that could calm the disturbed presence trapped in the small stone room. Sometimes we must forsake all the logical, earthly solutions for problems that seem resistant to those solutions. Sometimes only a higher power—a supernatural power, if you will—can bring peace. Thus did those experiencing the maelstrom come to call in a priest.

The priest came and indeed confirmed that there was a spirit trapped inside the small room, desperate to emerge and move on. The ancient words were said; the holy water was sprinkled; the sign of the cross within the circle was placed upon the door. No other sounds were heard from the stone room.

But the family had had enough. Soon after they sold the house and moved. The house, with its cold stone room, now belongs to the Lutheran Seminary. If the spirit of the young soldier should somehow find itself locked in the room again, there will be a number of new people of the cloth available now who can help him find his way out again.

TOURIST SEASON IN THE OTHER WORLD

Vex not his ghost: O! let him pass...
—William Shakespeare, *King Lear*, Act V, scene iii

On the southern edge of Gettysburg rests a quaint stone building, owned during the Battle of Gettysburg by a man with the redundant name of Mr. George George. Historical records trace the one-story, field-stone house back to one of Gettysburg's earliest settlers, the Rev. Alexander Dobbin. Though several hundred paces away from the main house, the structure was probably part of the original Dobbin homestead, perhaps acting as a servants' quarters. It is, therefore, one of the oldest structures still standing in Gettysburg.

Looking from the Dobbin House to the south on present-day Steinwehr Avenue (formerly the Emmitsburg Road) toward the George George house, you can allow your imagination to wash away the two centuries which have passed since the Dobbins owned the land you stand upon. Allow, if you will, the frame houses and brick commercial structures between to melt, and observe the lush open fields and dirt road materialize again. For eighty years from the Dobbins' first settling, the earth and road remained pastoral and unchanged. Who can ever know the joys and sorrows that were born, lived, and died within the sturdy, cold walls of that little house? Grief too, no doubt, imbedded itself within those walls when children or parents died and left the structure filled with mourning.

Using your imagination again, you can perhaps see, late one June afternoon, dusty columns of blue cavalrymen come riding up the road, sabers clanking, nervous, and with that certain look men have in their faces when they know they are about to become far too intimate with death.

And on the forenoon of the next day, out from the heavy firing of two great armies engaged to the west of town, you'll see a forlorn group of soldiers, bringing mourning and grief, come again to this small stone house along the main road to Maryland. Their burden is what used to be Maj. Gen. John F. Reynolds, his earthly body with its handsome face upturned, sightless to the July heavens, emptied of his essence by a Confederate's one-ounce, .57 caliber minie ball. His loyal aide, Charles Henry Veil, remembered with sadness the event: "The ball had entered the back of his neck, just over the coat collar, and passed downward in its course. The wound did not bleed externally and, as he fell, his coat collar had covered the wound, which accounted for my not discovering it at first. With the assistance of the men I found, we carried the body across the fields over to the

Emmitsburg Road, the one we had marched in on that morning...we carried his body to the little stone house on the Emmitsburg Road and laid it on the floor in the little sitting room."[1]

For a while, in the George family's field-stone house, the curtains are drawn and the general's body rests in the little sitting room while his loyal aides leave on the task of finding a suitable coffin.

Coffins are hard to find on this tumultuous day in Gettysburg. Up until the first horrid day of July 1863, Death was an infrequent caller to this town of about 2,400 souls. Suddenly, however, Death was the unwelcome visitor who wouldn't leave. Instead of a coffin, all Reynolds' aides could find was the box one was delivered in. They took it, but it was too short, and they had to break out one end so the general's body would fit.

Soon Reynolds would be taken to Baltimore for embalming, then to Philadelphia to lie in state in his sister's home, then to Lancaster to be buried with great honor. But from just before noon on July 1 when his body was brought off the battlefield until that evening, the earthly remains of Maj. Gen. John Fulton Reynolds, highest-ranking Union officer to die in the battle lay like a common soldier within the cold stone walls of the Georges' house.

Some say that, even today, if you enter the crawl space of the George George house, you may see the life's blood of the great general stained deep into the ancient wood on the underside of the floorboards and along the joists. Some of General Reynolds remains in Gettysburg into our day. Others have told of even stranger evidence of the man's passing, evidence that shows, perhaps, that he is not quite all gone from the town he helped make famous, and which repaid him with death.

Over the years, the George George house finally became part of the twentieth century. Though still quaint in its design and retaining much of its historic ambience, it has been rented out at various times to entrepreneurs of the tourist industry to be filled with relics and souvenirs of the battle. One couple opened a craft shop in the building and filled the place with counters and shelves and put pegboards on the walls to hold the various crafts.

One summer morning, two women entered the shop. They attracted the attention of the shopkeepers with their strange behavior. Pointing at the walls and murmuring between themselves, they wore looks of confusion. They left the building and the shopkeepers saw them walking back and forth, looking at the front of the house peeking in the windows, still with confused looks on their faces. Reentering the stone house, they continued to act confused, peering at the contents of the shop. Finally, one of the shopkeepers asked if he could help them.

"Where are the wax figures?" they asked.

"What wax figures?" he replied.

"The wax figures that were in this room last night."

The shopkeepers looked at each other.

"I'm sorry," one of them replied, "We don't have any wax figures in here. We've never had any wax figures here; just crafts and a few souvenirs."

"That's strange. We were walking around late last night and passed this house. We stopped and looked in that front window. The room was empty except for a woman dressed all in black sitting over there," she pointed to a corner filled with crafts, "in a rocking chair. Right in front of her," she pointed to a spot where a counter stood, "was a cot. Lying on the cot was a man, dressed in something dark. The woman looked like she was in mourning. The man seemed... dead."

The shopkeepers smiled politely. "Are you sure this was the shop you looked in last night? As you can see, the place is filled with crafts. We've never had any wax figures in here. You must be mistaken."

"No," said the other woman. "This is the place. Over there," she pointed to a wall covered with a pegboard and hanging crafts, "over there in that wall was a door. It must be behind that pegboard. Is there a door there?"

The shopkeepers were suddenly taken aback. Indeed, in the back wall, covered over by a pegboard several months before, was a door, original to the old stone building, but unseen since it had been covered by the need for hanging space.

The sudden and temporary rip in time between this world and the next can apparently happen at any moment, in any space. When it happens through a normal portal, like a door or window however, it seems even more a part of the reality in which we exist.

The George George house, Steinwehr Avenue

17

ACTORS OR REENACTORS

There must be ghosts all over the world.
They must be as countless as grains of the sands, it seems to me.
And we are so miserably afraid of the light, all of us.
—Henrik Ibsen, *Ghosts*, Act II

The experience of collecting well over one hundred stories of the paranormal experiences on and around the Gettysburg Battlefield sometimes seems very much like a sociological study in that certain patterns have emerged. One pattern is that whenever there is a change in the physical state of a place with historic significance, that is when psychic activity seems to be at its peak.

We can see it whenever someone restores a historic house. Numerous unexplainable events occur when old walls are being altered and ancient wood is given to the saw.

Bud and Carol Buckley, who beautifully restored the historic Cashtown Inn, saw what they believed to be a Confederate soldier standing in the doorway between the old part of the house and a newer section. Not once, but several times they saw him, as if he were inspecting their handiwork. Above their heads in the dark of the night from their bedroom, they heard heavy items being slid across the attic floor. Morning inspections always showed that not a thing had been moved.

When the restorations to the building which once beheld the passing of the magnificent rebel army were complete, the activity nearly stopped. Nearly, but not quite.

Other houses that felt the great pull of history from the whirlpool that was the Gettysburg Campaign have also shown an increase of paranormal activity when restoration-minded individuals have begun their work. A private home south of Gettysburg displayed several manifestations of unexplainable events to its owners as they were restoring it.

The owner is a historian and former professor at West Point and is currently director at the Center for the Study of the Civil War. The house pre-dates the Civil War. Union cavalry no doubt passed the house, since scouting every byway was standard operating procedure for cavalry. The Union Army's 11th Corps marched within a half-mile of the house on its way into the maelstrom that was to become the Battle of Gettysburg. Someone found the tip of a bayonet scabbard in his garden. There is documentation that an ordnance train from the 6th Corps parked on the property for a while during the battle. Karyol Kirkpatrick, a psychic, felt that much of the energy, however, predates the war.

During a visit Karyol felt that there was an "alley" of energy to the east of the house, as if a whirlwind or storm had come through there. She felt a woman being "hit"—perhaps by a tree or by lightning attracted to the tree. The woman, she felt, was a horsewoman, and may have been riding when it happened. As Karyol mentioned this, the woman who owns the house said that she had often gone into the barn and seen the normally calm horses suddenly spook for no reason at all. Karyol thought that there might be a connection between the dead woman's spirit and the stable she once frequented.

The owners of the house recall that much of the activity occurred while they were restoring or remodeling parts of the house. The bathroom in particular seems to be a center of high psychic activity. One night, the children were upstairs preparing to bathe before going to bed. Suddenly they came running down the stairs, panic-stricken, yelling something about having watched as the shower curtain wrapped itself completely around the shower rod. Both parents inspected the curtain. Between the looks of panic on their small children's faces, and the way the curtain was wrapped tightly around the rod, out of the children's reach, they realized that there was no possible way the kids could have accomplished the task.

Whatever it is in the bathroom seems to enjoy teasing little children. The two children would be upstairs and suddenly the water would be turned on. The same thing happened to an unsuspecting young nephew. The window curtain in the bathroom has been seen being pushed out into the room as if someone were behind it or some strong breeze had blown against it. The children and their mother have all witnessed the phenomenon. She confirmed that indeed, while the curtain was actively moving into the room, the window was closed.

There is a door just off the children's bedroom that opens and closes by itself. Before the couple moved in to the house, before there was even any furniture inside, the woman was upstairs and watched as the door between what was to become the children's bedroom and another bedroom slowly opened and then closed by itself.

On several occasions the couple found that the heat had been turned way up. The children were questioned but neither had touched the thermostat. The affected thermostat was in the children's room on the second floor, seemingly a vortex of spiritual energy.

Once, the couple had heard banging on the second floor; bolting upstairs the husband was about to tell the children to quiet down, but they were already quiet—sound asleep in their beds. Their confused, sleepy eyes told their father that they certainly were not the source of the banging. It is in this room where the door opens and closes by itself. It was also in this room that their youngest son continually had horrible nightmares. He doesn't sleep in that room anymore. "He hates that room," said his mother. The youngest in the household—the most vulnerable—hates the upstairs entirely.

And there were even stranger noises emerging from the second floor. Everyone in the family was downstairs watching TV. They remember that it was a Saturday night and after 11:30 p.m. Suddenly they heard what could only be described as a heavy stomping all across the second floor, "from one side of the house to the other." The man was so convinced that he had heard an intruder that he grabbed one of the Civil War sabers in his collection and ran upstairs to confront the intruder. No one was there. Although he hasn't heard the stomping sound since, she has, often enough to be teased by her husband about it.

Once, on the other side of the house, just a week after the family had moved in, the woman was in the house by herself, cleaning the back bathroom. She heard the heavy stomping around the upstairs, and for a moment was afraid that someone had broken into the house. She looked out of the bathroom and saw the shadow of a man on the wall. Curiosity overcame her fear and she went to see who it was. As she approached, the shadow vanished, but the family dog was sitting, staring at the space from where the shadow would have been cast, growling. Completely unnerved, the woman left the house.

During a visit to the second floor, Karyol distinctly felt that there was a column of energy—a vortex, if you will—leading directly through both floors and into the cellar. After Karyol left the second floor, a reporter for *The Gettysburg Times* who was covering Karyol's visit walked into the area between the children's beds and said she could feel something strange—like a concentration of static electricity—in an area about eighteen inches in diameter. As she stood in the spot I noticed that her legs were vibrating—as fast as a shiver produced by a cold chill—but not the same motion. She stepped from between the beds and we went downstairs. I asked her about her legs shaking.

"My legs were shaking?" she asked, incredulous.

"You didn't feel it?" I responded.

"You're kidding. My legs were shaking? I didn't know that."

She kept talking about the event, and made me describe exactly how her legs were moving. She hadn't felt it at all.

After Karyol's visit, the wife had an opportunity to do a little research. The family who owned the house just before the Civil War were the Cromers. In 1858 a 14-year-old girl, Sarah Cromer, was tragically killed in a horseback riding accident. The owners speculate that this might be the young horsewoman Karyol spoke of who causes the horses to spook inexplicably.

Even more bizarre was that one Walter Cromer was injured during the Civil War, wounded or (the records are unclear) perhaps kicked by a horse in the leg. Did the animal who kicked him partially cripple him, inflicting a lifelong limp? Or, like thousands and thousands of others hit in the leg by a minie ball, did he suffer through an amputation, and was he forced to stomp his way on a wooden leg through the rest of his—and perhaps this—life?

But the strangest occurrence involved the second floor hallway. The husband was working there when his eye was attracted to the end of the hall. There, on the original bathroom door was, as he described it, a "luminescent glow," "a phosphorescent spot or rather, a ball of light." So unusual did the light appear that he was compelled to walk to it to see where the source of the light was coming from. He looked for a round hole in the wall or window shade for the source, but there was none. He moved his hand completely around the circle of light but cast no shadow on it; the light seemed to be its own source. He went to touch it...and it vanished, an elusive remnant of some unknown and unexplained energy.

Though he believes that there is something to supernatural phenomena, he did not feel uncomfortable, and had no eerie feelings—just wonder at what this disappearing light with no source might have been.

Evidence of this heightened activity when restoration is taking place occurred on a large scale during the encampment of the reenactors who participated in the filming of the movie "Gettysburg." Several thousand authentically dressed Union and Confederate reenactors lived like soldiers, some of them for two months, in the summer of 1992 in the fields just west of Gettysburg National Military Park. For a while they actually "restored" the fields of Gettysburg to the way they looked nearly thirteen decades before.[1]

Historically the area was the rear of the Confederate lines where wounded were taken, supplies were kept, and troops were reorganized in preparation for going into battle. After the armies left, the land returned to its original use as grazing land or perhaps farm fields and remained that way until the summer of 1992, when once again it was populated with thousands of soldiers preparing for a different kind of war.

Suppose that our glimpses into the spiritual world—our "ghost" sightings—are not just a one-way view. Suppose, as some of the events documented appear to show that, as we can see them, they can see us. Could it be possible that as these thousands of authentically dressed soldiers assembled upon the fields of conflict in 1992, that other entities from another time, when the battlefield was first filled with soldiers, were looking out across time and watching?

Security was tight as the reenactors bedded down for the night upon their wool blankets and straw. Security guards watched through the darkness so that no local pranksters, or even tourists, would disturb the "background artists." It was late one sultry night, long after lights out for the reenactors. Though some would venture into town for dinner or drinks, they always carried their background artist badge to display upon reentering the compound.

The security guard's attention was drawn to a looming figure approaching through the dark. As it drew closer the guard realized that it was a man on horseback. He was dressed as a Confederate cavalryman and the horse wore the tack of one of the rangy Southern "roadsters" so popular in the Confederate cavalry. Assuming it was one of the background artists, but confused as to why he would be riding his horse around in the dark, he rose and approached the mounted figure. "May I see your background artists's badge, please?" was his question to the man. In return he got merely a quizzical look. Then the figure and his noble warhorse dematerialized before the befuddled eyes

21

of the security guard, apparently finished with his scouting mission into the right camp but in the wrong time.

The guard abruptly resigned his position.

One night well before dawn, one of the reenactors was sleeping in his car. It was a particularly cool night, and though his tent was nearby, he curled up in his vehicle to get away from the clammy morning air. He was awakened by the sounds of metal clanking and the soft clopping of hooves walking next to his car and tent. Reenactor Eric Johnson, who chronicled many of these events, remembered his words: "I thought it was a reenactor waking people up in a novel new way; then I looked at my watch. It was 3:17 a.m. I looked in the direction of the noise to observe a Confederate officer on a horse. I knew it was an officer because he had the piping—sometimes called 'chicken guts'—on his sleeve. He also had on a slouch hat." Slightly perturbed at being awakened so early, the man in the car began to open his door to find out what the "reenactor" was doing waking people up at quarter past three in the morning. When the car door opened and the light came on, the Confederate officer simply vanished.

The man closed the car door, extinguishing the light so that he could see better in the dark. He looked all about, but saw nothing.

Interestingly enough, when conversation about the incident came up the next day, at least three other people camping in tents nearby piped up and said yes, they too had heard the noises, a little after three in the morning but didn't look to see what it was. But they were certain of what they heard: the unmistakable sounds of horses' hooves clopping by, and the rhythmic rattle of a Civil War sabre against a horse's tack.

Reenactors particularly dislike thunderstorms. Not only do they make them miserable in their little canvas "dog tents," but they provide a real danger to men outdoors in soaked uniforms and wet leather shoes holding what is essentially a very efficient lightning rod—a musket with a bayonet attached. Historically, lightning strikes on marching columns of men did occur, sometimes with fatal results. No less a personage than Maj. Gen. Joshua L. Chamberlain wrote in *Passing of the Armies* of just such an event as the Army of the Potomac returned to Washington in the spring of 1865, after the surrender at Appomattox:

> In the middle of the afternoon a heavy rainstorm swept over us, opening with terrific summons of thunder and lightning, sky and earth meeting. I chanced to be at that moment on the summit of a very high hill, from which I could see the whole corps winding its caravan with dromedary patience. The first lightning-bolt nearly stunned me. I saw its forerunner flashing along the cannon far ahead and illuminating Crawford's column with unearthly glare; and turning quickly towards my own I could see the whole black column struggling on and Ayres a mile behind urging and cheering his men...when this ever-recurrent pulse of flame leaped along the writhing column like a river of fire. It looked to me as if the men had bayonets fixed, the points of intense light flew so sharp from the muzzles sloping above the shoulders. Suddenly an explosion like a battery of shrapnel fell right be-

tween our divisions. An orderly came galloping up to me, with word that one of the ambulances was struck, killing the horses and the driver, and stunning the poor fellows who, unable to keep up with the rushing column, had sought this friendly aid.[2]

No reenactor is foolish enough to march around in a thunderstorm. One night during the first few days of August a typical summer thunderstorm with lightning, rolling thunder, and a solid wall of rain advanced, like some infernal army, from the hills to the west across the encampment site. A lone reenactor ventured from his tent out into the night to watch the majesty of the battle in the sky, and was surprised and a little shocked to see a battalion-size group of Confederate infantry forming up in line and coming to attention across the road from the camp. He called to some of his friends in the surrounding tents and those who peeked out saw the same thing: uniformed men, seemingly driven by foolishness, or an inconceivably strong devotion which appeared to conquer even the fear of death by lightning strike, to reenact a Civil War era scene. They could be seen clearly through the rain, but even more distinctly during the lightning flashes, adjusting their ranks with military fastidiousness, as if in nervous preparation for battle. The men in the tents watched. They saw the battalion finally aligned; a great flash of lightning illuminated them one more time. As the observers' eyes adjusted to the darkness after the flash, they saw that the unit was gone—vanished in an instant, called suddenly into some unseen combat, crossing through time's illusionary wall.

Though the timing is uncertain, either shortly before or after this event, a lone Confederate battalion was seen, in swinging route step, marching along one of the camp roads through the Union campsite. Was it the same group seen in the field outside the camp? For that matter, was this phantom battalion perhaps the same one seen by dignitaries on Little Round Top years before? Or the one that continues to be seen to this day near where battalions of live men were mown like so much grass in the once-deadly Wheatfield?

There was the pastor—a minister in real life who reenacts as a man of the cloth—who had gone out of the campsite to get something out of the trunk of his car. It was around 10:30 p.m. and most of the reenactors had bedded down after a sunrise-to-sunset schedule of shooting the film. As the pastor was moving things about in his trunk, he felt a sudden uneasiness, as if he were being watched. Turning, he saw that he was virtually surrounded by a company-size group of what he thought were reenactors. But the looks on their faces seemed to indicate serious work ahead. Inconceivable as it was—for reenactors are by nature nice people—he felt as if he were about to be attacked. Nervously he asked, "What's the problem here?" The entire group slowly melted away, back into that strange land where there is apparently no leave from duty for those soldiers caught there. The pastor realized that he had missed an incredible opportunity: the chance to help these men, *en masse*, to find their eternal rest.

And restless a few of them were indeed. About three-and-a-half hours later, at 2 a.m., one of the reenactors was at the phone bank calling his wife on the West

Coast. The conversation went on as they discussed with her when he'd be coming home. He wanted to stay in Gettysburg for more of the filming and figured he'd be home in a few more days, or perhaps as long as a week. Over his shoulder he saw several men in uniform behind him whom he hadn't noticed before. He told his wife that he must go now because there were others waiting to use the phone. He looked back at them and, as he stood listening to his wife ask again when he was coming home, they simply dematerialized. There was an uneasy silence coming from his end of the line until he finally answered his wife: "I'll be coming home tomorrow."

Apparitions come to us through many senses. Visual apparitions are only the most dramatic. There have been a number of olfactory apparitions around the battlefield and town of Gettysburg as well. Tobacco, years before its deadly effects were known, was used liberally by both Yankee and Rebel. With over 160,000 troops in the vicinity, it is no wonder that certain walkers upon the battlefield claim that, even though no one else is anywhere near them, they seem to have suddenly walked into a cloud of acrid tobacco smoke.

One of the main components of the black powder used during the war was sulfur. During a Civil War battle the air was thick with the smell of burning sulfur, smelling for all the world like rotten eggs. There, on the fields today occasionally a visitor will crinkle his nose, appalled at the hellish smell, and will look in vain for where some eggs may have been left to rot. Like the hell-on-earth it once signaled, the fire-and-brimstone smell rifts again across the fields of war.

Occasionally too, across the clean, fresh fields, or within the pristine houses of the townspeople who just happen to live on what was once battlefield, comes the hideous stench of putrefying flesh. This smell was once so common shortly after those three terrible days in July that Gettysburgians almost constantly wore masks soaked in oil of wintergreen to filter the fetidness of death. It has been written about before, and since that writing, people confirm that occasionally it rolls in again from beyond the fields, from beyond the present time.

And there are the assaults upon the ears that seem to be very common—and very out-of-place—upon the now peaceful battlefield. Just outside the encampment for the filming of "Gettysburg," some reenactors reported hearing twice the discharge of cannons. Walking to where the cannons were "parked" they examined them and realized that none had been fired recently; none showed the telltale grime of black powder discharge or smelled of the sulfur in the black powder.

During the filming of the scene at Devil's Den, after all was quiet, from the thick woods across Bloody Run on the slope of Big Round Top came the unmistakable sound of two cannons discharging and the crackle of scattered musketry. It was as if the spirits of the patriotic slain rose from the earth, fooled into thinking they were needed once more to fight and die yet again.

While walking through the Wheatfield where 6,000 men were beaten down by the uncaring fist of combat, a lone reenactor was taking in the evening air. Faintly across the field wafted the sounds of a drummer-boy, still rapping the men into battle, rhythmically, closer and closer toward death.

It was late in the fall, after most of the reenactors had gone home to their jobs and families, that a handful remained to help out the camera crews if they needed it. Again near Devil's Den, some reenactors lounged about after all the others had gone back to the base camp, and quiet descended with the sun on the greatest battlefield on the North American continent. They heard, on the gentle breeze coming from the thick woods near Big Round Top, men talking. Then, familiar to them as they were familiar to their forbearers, across the valley came the old tunes of the war—"Lorena," "The Bonnie Blue Flag," or perhaps the soldiers' favorite "Home Sweet Home,"—sung by men who had been trying but were unable to find their way home again after 130 years of uneasy sleep.

A young woman wrote to tell of her experience with the 6th New Hampshire reenactment regiment on the 130th anniversary of the great battle. They were encamped on the 4th of July not too far from the wooded area in the campsite. It was a week of record high temperature in Gettysburg, aggravated by the lack of any breeze on that particular night. She and a few of the regiment were gathered around the cooking fire, finishing off some dinner. Suddenly, one of the men stopped eating and cocked an ear. "Listen," he said. He stood, looking toward the darkened woodline. As the others stopped eating and put down their plates, from the woods came the unmistakable sounds of a large body of troops moving. There was the clatter and clank of bayonets against canteens, the rattle and murmur of thousands of men shifting and adjusting personal things like packs and rifles, the low rumble of what sounded like a wagon, and random but rhythmic shuffle of feet as men moved wearily through the woods.

The reenactors looked at each other with anxiety—they all heard it. One nervously suggested that it was only the wind, but his theory was belied by the motionless, oppressive heat around them and the campfire smoke rising in a straight column. From less than a hundred yards away—the young woman thought the sounds came as close as only fifty yards at one time—echoed the rumble of an invisible army. The sounds apparently came so close that some-one in the group nervously suggested that perhaps they should go for a walk to another part of the large campsite. Though no one admitted it at the time, the young woman later frankly said that the stroll was prompted not so much for the exercise, but by fear.

In the several pages recounting paranormal activities at the re-enactment sent by Eric Johnson there is the cryptic note on page two: "Date unknown. Supply wagon heard going thru [sic] camp."

Late one night on the site that had been constructed to look just like the famous angle—the High Water Mark of the Confederacy—someone saw a lone campfire flickering near the exact replica of terrain that saw so much bloodshed. The reenactor found a friend. Then they found two security guards. Obviously, some reenactors were camping in an unauthorized area and presenting a fire danger, since the summer had been hot and fairly dry. As the four of them approached the site, the flames began to flicker lower and lower and finally disappeared as they approached to within several yards of the spot. They walked directly to the site to make sure that the fire that had been burning was indeed completely out. Strangely, as they reached the site, there was no sign of a fire—no burned embers or smoldering earth or smoking firepit. There had never been a fire where they had so recently just seen one.

Another brief note in Eric's manuscript states, "Security guards investigate 'men with torches' at the corner of the camp." Could this be the same event, or perhaps another, like the numerous fires sometimes seen along the South Mountain range where the Confederates once camped, or the fires seen in the Wheatfield that also left no ashes?

Since even Hollywood cannot recreate some of the fabulous terrain where heroes fought and died at Gettysburg, some of the scenes for the movie were to be shot "on location," on the battlefield where the events the reenactors were portraying actually took place. The reenactors' reaction to being able to do this was beyond ecstatic: most felt a deep reverence and were sincerely honored to be able to march, literally, in the footsteps of their heroes.

It was late summer when they were to film the reenactment of that great conflagration of souls known to history as Pickett's Charge. The day was sultry with the temperature approaching the 90s as the men lined up along Seminary Ridge. Modern reenactors are relatively savvy about the event in history they are about to portray. No doubt, some of them were remembering their history as they stood and sweated under some of the same trees that once sheltered those who, a century and a third before, were soon to leave orphans behind and were themselves about to be adopted by Death.

Perhaps they thought of the two hour cannonade preceding the charge and the story of poor Jere Gage of the 11th Mississippi, lying with his arm nearly torn off by a Federal shell. When the surgeon approached to look at his arm, the boy told him, "Doctor, that isn't where I am hurt," and pulled back the blanket to reveal that there was nothing left of his abdomen. Before he took opium to ease the pain, however, he wrote a note to his mother and sisters and released "Miss Mary" from some personal promise. He dipped the finished letter in his mortal wounds, consecrating it with his own blood.[3]

Perhaps some of them recalled Federal artilleryman Alonzo Cushing, mutilated in the crotch and thighs by a shell doubly cruel to a young man, as he walked up to his commander holding what was left of himself together with his hand. Brig. Gen. Webb may have thought he was about to request to go to the rear, but perhaps feeling that now there was little to live for, young Cushing asked if he could place his guns at the wall and fight to the finish. Webb knew what he was asking for, and granted his request. Cushing took a bullet in the mouth a short time later and got his wish.[4]

The heat was stifling as the reenactors stepped off across the broad plain. As anyone who has crossed the field of Pickett's Charge knows, it is not as flat as it appears. Especially near the Virginia monument, the land dips and rolls into several swales. They marched along the same route where men were liquified by exploding shells or bashed to the ground by concussion, without a mark on them, dead. They maneuvered over ground where entire lines of men were obliterated by crossfire from the batteries on Little Round Top, whose gunners thought the firing was as easy as target practice.

Over the crest of one of the little ridges and down again they marched, dropping into a little valley where they could no longer see cameras or directors or modern film crews. Suddenly, from the stifling heat of the modern field of Hollywood recreations, they plunged into the frosty cold of another world. It was as if the entire marching line had walked into a deep freeze at the bottom of that swale. Individuals began to look around at the others to see if they were experiencing the same thing; indeed the incredulity upon each face told them they had passed into someplace not of this world. Some swore they saw their own and other's breath condensing in the cold air. Then it was up the other side and back into the hell-like heat of the sun-beaten field. They finished their march and the filming, but with a renewed respect for the undeniable and unpredictable power of the unknown.

And finally, from the camp where modern reenactors so faithfully and convincingly portrayed the long-gone battle's counterfeit, comes the story of a local who was contracted to shuttle the reenactors to and from the town. This woman owned a pick-up truck and had just driven some "soldiers" into Gettysburg from the campsite and was returning. It was one of those fog-filled nights so common on the battlefield, where the mist assembles itself in long, militarily precise lines, then stands, as if at attention, across the road to Emmitsburg, or Fairfield, or Cashtown, in mocking imitation of real lines of infantry cut down in those exact spots.

The woman was returning to the reenactors' campsite with her empty truck to see if there was another group that needed a lift. She had been driving non-stop through that strange fog and was still a few miles from the camp when she began to hear a tapping that she described as coming from the truck bed or perhaps the roof just above her head.

She looked in the rear-view mirror. The mirror gave her something more than just a look back from where she had come; it suddenly was looking back in time, for there, in the formerly empty bed of the truck, were several Civil War-era soldiers. They sat, half a dozen historical anachronisms, weary and tattered, riding from the town where the woman had just dropped off their imitators, back out into the darkened fields of sacrifice more familiar to them than the neon-lighted modern town of Gettysburg. They said not a word, but just stared with that strange look in their eyes—the "thousand-yard stare," they would call it in a later war—or as one poet put it, with the sad eyes of a newborn beast of burden.

The camp where the guards and the rest of the reenactors were located seemed a hundred miles away. The battlefield is a very dark place at night and the roads that wind through the various sites of hideous combat can be very lonely. She didn't want to look again in that rear-view mirror, yet still, from somewhere, came that rhythmic, continuous tapping, tapping. Suddenly, ahead of her through the fog, were campfires. It was the encampment. She swerved into the driveway and up to the guard at the gate. Still apprehensive about the timeless cargo she thought she was carrying, she quickly asked the guard if there was anyone in the bed of her truck. He answered no. Had any reenactors been seen jumping out and tumbling to the ground as she sped to the guard shack? Again the answer that belied reality and confirmed the paranormal. No. There had been no re-enactors jumping from the swiftly moving truck.

If it were only that easy to peer into a looking-glass and see across time at soldiers so wearied by combat and the heavy burden of being caught forever in a certain place and at a certain time that they are willing to take a ride on even so strange a horseless wagon.

ALONE IN HELL

A stranger has come
To share my room in the house not right in the head...
— Dylan Thomas, "Love in the Asylum"

The summer that seemed to have no end in Gettysburg finally passed. The gathering of the wounded was over. The burying of the dead (then reburying, after the rains had washed open the shallow graves) went on and on through July, then August, then September, and October 1863.

First, the noble dead were gathered together and interred near where they fell. Soon, however, local farmers were saddled with the onerous task of caring for the graves when the weather exposed a grisly body part or when animals disturbed the final slumber of some unfortunate son of the North or South. They also had to plow around the makeshift sepulchers. It wasn't long before the cries went up to the state capital in Harrisburg to find a better resting-place for these men. The price the soldiers paid for their little bit of Pennsylvania real estate apparently wasn't high enough for the local farmers.

Gettysburg attorney David Wills was authorized to purchase land for the reinterment of the sainted—but unwanted—Union dead. He looked to Cemetery Hill, where the Evergreen Cemetery was already located, and bought land there. Soon, the work of exhumation was begun and the farmers were much happier.

On through the autumn the gravediggers worked, with their long iron hooks, going through the soldiers' pockets for any indication—a letter, an engraved watch, a rare identification tag—that might tell who these crumbling shells once were. Carefully—when they could—they lifted the ragged, sodden uniforms from the earth and placed them into wooden coffins, then carried them to Cemetery Hill, there to be laid in a giant semi-circle, feet facing inward. Attorney Wills realized that a new cemetery, especially one containing so many soldiers, would need a dedication. Acclaimed orator Edward Everett accepted the invitation to speak, but requested that the October date be extended to November. The 19th of that month was agreed upon.

With the main orator scheduled to his own convenience, Wills then wrote to the President of the United States—some six weeks after Everett's invitation and just two weeks before the event was to occur. As one of the commissioners remembered long after, "the question was raised as to his [Lincoln's] ability to speak on such a grave and solemn occasion."

Wills' invitation to Lincoln clearly tells Lincoln his place in the ceremonies and indicates the concern of the commissioners that he might, if allowed to speak too long, say something foolish: "It is the desire that after the oration, you, as Chief Executive of the Nation, formally set apart these grounds to their sacred use by a few appropriate remarks."[1]

Of course, Lincoln could not have chosen any more appropriate remarks than those he did choose. Everett spoke for two hours; Lincoln for less than two minutes. It is one of the curiosities of the American character that the shorter speech is the one most remembered and most beloved.

Lincoln spent the night polishing the address in the front bedroom of the Wills' house. He spoke briefly to a crowd gathered below, then went back to work, honing and fretting over the two-page speech. Much was on the line, and Lincoln knew it. He had been accused of making crude jokes while touring the Antietam Battlefield near Sharpsburg, Maryland, the autumn before. One can only wonder what marvelous, worrisome energy poured out of this inherently melancholy man as he worked the words with which he hoped not to merely dedicate a cemetery, but to rededicate a war-weary nation to continue the sacrifice for a higher good. One can only wonder as well, with Lincoln's own predisposition toward the paranormal, and the intense emotional energy expended in that building, whether some of the martyred President remains.

The David Wills house on Lincoln Square

There is a lock of Lincoln's hair encased on display in the Wills' House Museum. Karyol Kirkpatrick, a psychic, visited the Wills' House in 1994 and was taken to the lock to feel the psychic vibrations from the monumental human being to which the hair once belonged. Of all things in Gettysburg associated with Lincoln, surely this must contain some of the vital spark that was once within the man. She passed her hand over the relic, once, twice, again, and turned to shake her head: nothing. She felt no power or energy coming from a most rare and intimate item associated with Abraham Lincoln.

Of course not. The lock was taken from Lincoln's head during the postmortem examination—the autopsy—after John Wilkes Booth's lead Derringer ball had carved its savage way through Lincoln's brain, taking with it all that was the man on this earth. When told where the lock had come from, Karyol smiled and nodded. That's why she felt nothing from the hair—Lincoln was already dead, his spirit on another journey, when this small bit of him was clipped.

But others who work at the Lincoln Room Museum swear at the evidence they hear occasionally of the great man's presence, recurring in the building where his mind polished one of the greatest speeches in the history of humankind.

Lincoln has been seen, heard, and felt, of course, walking the halls of the White House in Washington, D.C., dozens and dozens of times and documented by such no-nonsense people as Grace Coolidge and Presidents Theodore Roosevelt, Dwight D. Eisenhower, and that noted cynic from the "Show-me" state, Harry Truman. Valets and secretaries to other presidents have literally seen Lincoln, as did Queen Wilhelmina of the Netherlands.[2]

Apparently, he revisits Gettysburg too. During the "off season" in Gettysburg, visitors to the Wills' House are few and far between. Yet when there are no visitors in the building, attendants in the reception room of the Lincoln Room Museum can hear the rhythmic creaking of the wood floors in the bedroom and in the museum room itself, as if someone were composing a piece of writing—or perhaps practicing a speech out loud—and pacing back and forth absentmindedly while doing so, or standing to walk and stretch from being hunched over a desk and paper too long.

Apprehensively, the attendants will emerge from behind the information desk and walk into the museum room to see for themselves if a visitor they had missed had come in. They walk as well into the Lincoln bedroom, only to find that they are seemingly alone—physically alone, at least—and that no one apparent to the human eye is with them.

Some who have rented the apartment on the top floor of the Wills' House have heard it as well: the footsteps on the floor below, late at night, or early into the morning hours, after the museum has been long-closed and even the center square of Gettysburg is quiet.

On November 19, 1863, the parade to the cemetery began in front of David Wills' home, on the "diamond," the name for the center square of town during the nineteenth century. Anyone familiar with Gettysburg knows that it only takes fifteen minutes to get from the square to the cemetery on the outskirts of town—and that's on horseback. So it was then.

In the little vale between what locals call Baltimore Hill and Cemetery Hill, sits a house Lincoln and the entourage rode past on that morning. From its location between the opposing Union and Confederate lines during the battle, the building witnessed not only the passing of a great President but had seen the comings and goings of both Federal and Rebel during and after the battle. And it seems that there have been some more recent comings and goings as well.

The lovely, balconied house had been built in 1819, and remarkably, its appearance has hardly changed in over 175 years. During the battle, no doubt Confederate skirmishers were actively engaged in and around the house. After the battle, when the Confederate line retreated from the town, Union soldiers cautiously entered the yard and, curious, probably explored the house. The building even appears in historic photos taken four months later, showing President Lincoln riding to deliver the Gettysburg Address.

At the time of the battle, the house was part of John Winebrenner's tannery. After it had remained a private residence for many years, it became a business once again: an art gallery in the 1990s. One of the people working in the gallery had decorated the mantle in the front room with figurines—cold-cast canteens, small figures, toy soldiers, and antiques—setting them "just so,"

The procession to the Soldiers' National Cemetery, November 19, 1863.
(Library of Congress)

the way she thought they looked best. She would lock up at night, but when she returned early the next morning to reopen, the soldiers, canteens, and other militaria had been rearranged. Carefully, she placed them back in the order in which she wanted them.

A week or so later as she was opening the gallery, she noticed that the figures had been rearranged again. She began replacing them the way she liked them. But while she was rearranging them she got what she described as a "cold, cold, *cold*, damp cold" feeling on her right side, even though it was a sunny, warm morning. While she was working at the mantle, her eye was drawn to the one door at the far end of the house—a door they never opened, and kept sealed for security reasons. There she saw, coming *through* the closed, solid door, the figure of a man. Astounded, she watched as he slowly materialized, his foot and leg and the front of his body first, then his profile, then, slowly, his back. She described him as wearing a short cape over a long, gray-blue coat. He wore high boots, a wide-brimmed hat, and a full, chest-length, brown beard. In his hands he carried gauntlets. As soon as he had passed completely through the door and entered the room, he disappeared. A few days later, she returned in the morning to open the gallery and noticed that her display on the mantle had been rearranged again and began replacing them. She looked apprehensively toward the sealed door, but saw nothing.

Once again, in another week, the soldiers and militaria had been rearranged. It was getting to be old hat: the mantle was rearranged repeatedly sometimes twice a month or more, almost as if someone disagreed with her tactical arrangement of the tiny troops in the battle of the mantle. It was a cold, overcast morning this time as she began to set up her display again. Suddenly she felt the chill begin to increase in intensity and looked hesitatingly through the house to the sealed door. Again, into the house came the figure she had seen once before, striding through a solid door, dressed in the uniform of a Civil War-era soldier, only to disappear once more before her eyes. She said that she felt no fear from his presence—although she admits to having been in houses where she had been very fearful of something present yet unseen. Instead, these times she felt that he seemed to be just "striding through, ready to do something."

Her daughter also had an unnerving experience. She was standing in the newer section of the house during a quiet time of the day. Suddenly she had a feeling that someone was watching her. She turned and looked toward the original front door of the old part of the house—the door on the south side of the structure—and there to her amazement stood a soldier dressed in a "cream-colored, butternut uniform," with long reddish or auburn hair and a scraggly beard and moustache. She described him as wearing a floppy, sweat-stained, butternut-colored hat. She saw he had a blanket roll on his back, attached across his chest with what she thought were canvas straps. He was very skinny and gaunt and very pale. She saw that he carried a long rifle, "almost as tall as he was," which seemed to her to be a good six feet. They stood and gazed directly into each other's eyes.

She recalled that it seemed he stood there for minutes, his direct gaze piercing hers, although upon reflection, she figured it may have been only 15 or 20 seconds. As he looked directly at her she said he wore an expression of extreme sadness in his eyes—so sad, in fact, that she actually felt his sadness. "It looked," she said "as if he'd really been through hell. He just looked at me as if to say, 'please help me,' or 'please feel sorry for me.'" She said she didn't feel threatened, just sad. Suddenly he was gone, dematerializing before her eyes.

Occasionally after that, she felt his presence, but never saw him again. But whenever she felt his presence, she felt safe, as if he were watching over her. One other feeling she had was that she felt as if he was "trapped" in the old kitchen area and could not move into the newer section of the building where she was.

Finally, after they sold the house, an insurance company bought it and began using it as offices. One of the female employees was working late one night, upstairs. She distinctly heard the door open and close; she heard footsteps moving around downstairs. At first she assumed it was her boss who had stopped by to pick up some work, since she knew all the doors had been locked. But the footsteps moved around rather aimlessly. Finally, she decided to go downstairs since she had a couple of questions for her boss anyway. As she descended the stairs, she heard the footfalls cease. As she reached the first floor, she realized that there was no one on the first floor. She quickly grabbed her work and bolted out of the door.

Two soldiers: one Union and one Confederate, one who may be stuck in time and locale, and one who may just be passing through. Both, seemingly having seen enough horrors when they were alive during the Civil War to wonder if they had been mistakenly ordered to Hell instead of Gettysburg, continue to visit, for some unresolved reason, the lovely old house on Baltimore Street.

HELL IS FOR CHILDREN, TOO

Thus she spoke; and I longed to embrace my mother's ghost.
Thrice I tried to clasp her image,
and thrice it slipped through my hands like a shadow,
like a dream.

—Homer, *The Odyssey*

The horror of Gettysburg did not end on the battlefield.

Like some insidious, ever-expanding plague, the effects of the thousands of casualties left moaning on the battlefield spread to virtually every large city and small crossroads in America. As the long lists were published in newspapers, mothers would kneel, pull their children to them and tearfully whisper, "Papa's not coming home from the war." The agony was cruelly non-partisan. North or South, it didn't matter. "He was killed at Gettysburg in Pennsylvania," was repeated over and over, before crude firesides and elegant marble mantles all across the country.

After two years of war, death was epidemic. Mothers were helpless without the meager money sent home from their soldier-husbands, and at a time before women worked out of the home. What to do with the children, orphaned and impoverished by this immense, unholy war?

A temporary solution was found when a mystery was solved.

Shortly after the Battle of Gettysburg, the stiffening corpse of a Union soldier was seen hunched in a sitting position near the railroad in an overgrown field where Stratton Street and the York Road intersect. Clutched in his hand was an ambrotype of three children. There was no other identification on his body. He had been hit by a minie ball in the chest just above the heart, and so had a precious few seconds of life left after the soft lead struck him. It was obvious what his last thoughts on earth were of: his precious children and their welfare without a father. He was buried near where he fell, but the ambrotype—and the story of how much it meant to him—was recovered and embraced by Dr. J. Francis Bourns, a wealthy Philadelphian who was serving as a volunteer surgeon.

Moved by the story of the unknown Union soldier whose last thoughts were of his children left behind, he had the ambrotype copied as *cartes de visite* and published in hope of identifying the soldier.

In Portville, New York, a woman had heard of the huge battle in south-central Pennsylvania. Ominously, at about the same time, like in thousands of other

Monument to Sgt. Amos Humiston and his children near where he fell

homes across the country, the letters from her husband, without explanation, simply ceased arriving.

Meantime, Dr. Bourns, with his own money, circulated the image throughout the country in various publications, including one called *The American Presbyterian.* One, and only one, resident of Portville was a subscriber and recognized the three children in the publication as those of her neighbor, Philinda Humiston, whose husband, Amos, was a soldier. The image was shown to Mrs. Humiston. She recognized her children, and realized the fate of her husband at that moment. Again the gathering of the children to her; again the awful words, "Papa's never coming home again."

The soldier was thus identified as Sgt. Amos Humiston of the 154th New York Infantry. Immediately it was thought that the sale of the moving photograph and its story would provide money to educate the Humiston children; it was also believed that enough money could be raised to establish an orphanage for the children of other deceased Union soldiers. Copies of the now-famous photo were sold, a poetry contest was held, and other fundraising efforts finally paid off. Gettysburg was chosen as the natural site for the National Orphan's Homestead, with Mrs. Humiston as its first matron. The building chosen in Gettysburg had been used as Gen. Oliver Otis Howard's headquarters during the battle.

The Homestead opened in the fall of 1866. Gen. Ulysses S. Grant visited in 1867. Shortly after its opening, the children began a tradition that continues on every Memorial Day to the present: laying flowers on the graves of the dead in the National Cemetery, just up the street. It seemed appropriate since many of the children had the sad duty of placing flowers on the graves of their own fathers, killed in the Battle of Gettysburg.

The orphanage did well until Mrs. Humiston remarried and resigned her position as matron. The arrival of a new matron, Mrs. Rosa Carmichael, signaled a change in the way things were run in the orphanage, and a descent into cruelties that no child deserved.

The tradition of the orphans strewing flowers on the graves of the dead ceased by order of Mrs. Carmichael. Imagine the orphans, on succeeding Memorial Days, watching the other children of Gettysburg lay flowers on the graves of their own fathers, while they, only a short walk away, were forced not to participate.

Other punishments were soon to follow. Stories slowly emerged of cruelty to the orphans: they were confined in a damp, dark hole in the cellar named "the dungeon"; they were placed in shackles and suspended by the arm in barrels. One brutal older orphan acted as kapo and kicked and beat the younger ones; a 5-year-old was discovered by a neighbor one bitterly cold Christmas Eve, screaming, locked in an outbuilding; a little girl was made to stand on a desk, balancing precariously until she nearly collapsed. Though others were beaten and kicked, all evidence disappeared when the inspectors came.

General U.S. Grant with others visited the National Homestead at Gettysburg in 1867.

After a bitter battle in the newspapers and the courts, the Homestead for Orphans of the Civil War was closed in 1877, never to be opened again. Mrs. Charmichael was sent packing, the children dispersed.

Some say, however, that they are not altogether gone.

The orphanage building became a museum to the Civil War soldier. Over the years, visitors to the museum have continued to report hearing the cries of children when in the Soldier's National Museum. As recently as three years ago, visitors heard the mournful, heartbreaking sounds of children screaming and crying seemingly coming from the back of the building or perhaps from the cellar where Mrs. Carmichael's dank "dungeon" once held youngsters in its damp embrace. An investigation by the management of the museum proved that no one else was in the building at the time, nor was anyone in the adjacent buildings. It was during the "off season" and all the other buildings nearby were closed.

Could it be these tortured children's souls crying out that were said to be heard at odd hours and random times in the National Cemetery Lodge—just two doors up from the orphanage—for years before this author moved into the Lodge? Could it have been one of these interminably damned children that I indeed heard crying out one dark night in the Lodge?[1]

As if their childhood wasn't stolen away from them soon enough by war's random, illogical brutality; as if having a dear father and his love wrenched away by far-off, heartless politics incomprehensible to children, wasn't the last straw. The children's spirits continue, apparently, to suffer through the ages and the generations, poignant reminders of the results of that most horrible offspring ever of man: war.[2]

BROTHERHOOD FOREVER

When the footpads quail at the night-bird's wail,
and black dogs bay at the moon,
Then is the specters' holiday—then is the ghosts' high noon!
—Sir Wm. Schwenck Gilbert, *Ruddigore*, Act II

College fraternities have a number of well-known reputations, some good, some bad. Gettysburg College's fraternities are no different, with the attributes of brotherhood, friendship, and service, as well as the notoriety of being the places to go for revelry on a Friday or Saturday night.

The Sigma Nu House on West Broadway is known for eerie footsteps, levitations, and the sounds of doors opening and closing when no one has entered or left.[1] Along with it are a number of other houses, once privately owned that now shelter fraternity men—and apparently some other beings as well....

The Theta Chi House stands on Carlisle Street. The house was built by Col. Charles H. Buehler.[2] Buehler, in his youth, attended Pennsylvania (now Gettysburg) College for two years and then became involved in publishing the local newspaper. When the Civil War broke out he enlisted and spent two years serving. Returning to Gettysburg after his service, he built the house in 1869, one of the first constructed north of the railroad.

Evidence of the ethereal nature of supernatural tales is the fact that the events that were said to have brought on the unexplainable occurances are often different in their beginnings. Obviously, the telling of tales through the generations can account for the differences. Two legends have emerged from the lore of the Theta Chi House, both of which revolve around the cellar, either of which could be the genesis for the strange happenings recorded over the years.

The first of the legends of the Theta Chi House records that many years ago, one of the brothers, in spite of health ordinances in Gettysburg proscribing certain quirky disposals of the dead, requested, and was granted his request, to be buried in the basement of the old house. Someone—perhaps some new brother who grew squeamish at the thought of a body sleeping eternally below where he slept—apparently reported this grisly last request and, in spite of the deceased's desire to spend eternity with "the brotherhood," the body was removed to a more appropriate cemetery and there laid to rest.

Shortly afterward, odd—and even bizarre—events began to take place in the house. Lights in a certain room would suddenly extinguish. A trip to the switch and a flick would turn them back on again. A query of other brothers would reveal that no other lights had flickered during that time indicating a power failure or blown fuse. It was as if someone simply wanted the lights off in just that room.

Creaking noises, sometimes like footsteps, sometimes like floorboards buckling, would emanate from halls and rooms when no one was there to make the noises. Rapping noises (which some researchers wish to attribute to interior pipes or tree limbs outside) were heard inside the house. Doors left open would slowly swing shut, even on windless days. These same doors, on other occasions, would slowly swing open, as if allowing someone out of the rooms. Student researchers have given excellent, documented explanations for most of the occurances, but some of the occupants are convinced that they are the manifestations of a fraternity member long dead who was first granted his deathbed wish—then had it taken away—to spend eternity with his brothers.

The second of the legends is that of a man named Thompson. Current research fails to indicate whether Thompson was an owner or just a tenant in the house. Either way, brothers in the 1980s called a room in the basement, "Thompson's Room," identified thus because it was in this room that the mysterious Thompson allegedly killed his wife and buried her. Thompson fled the area, but, like some character out of an Edgar Allen Poe story, he was driven to imprudent actions by his guilty conscience. He returned to Gettysburg, confessed his guilt, and, apparently deciding that official justice was not quick enough to suit his own nagging conscience, hanged himself.

From this second legend comes the documented story of how one of the brothers who graduated in 1980 had walked into the house and heard muffled voices coming fro run in the Orphanagem the room which is situated right above "Thompson's Room." Walking closer to the room he realized that the door was closed. He also realized that he did not recognize the voices as belonging to any of the brothers. He knocked on the door and the voices stopped. He opened the door, and to his astonishment, the room was empty.

Another brother was getting ready for bed and had turned off his light. He had crawled into bed and had begun to doze off when the light came back on. The switch was of a dimmer variety, the type one pushes to turn on the pushes to turn off again. He got out of bed, pushed the switch to turn off the lights and got back into bed. Just as he was nodding off, again the lights came back on. Finally, after turning the lights off a third time, they remained extinguished, though the student's imagination certainly burned more brightly after the incident.

Late in 1981 some of the brothers were partying in what they call the "Mystic Rites Room" on the third floor. Someone had brought up the topic of ghosts, and the discussion proceded in that direction for some time. Finally, one of the brothers excused himself to go to bed.

When he crawled into bed, his reading light was hanging on the wall behind his bunk, just beyond the side of his bed. The light had fallen from the nail a few times before, and always dropped straight down and landed on the floor. The next morning he awoke, rolled over, and found the lamp had come off the nail again. But this time, instead of crashing to the floor directly below, it was lying on the bed right next to him, placed there by some unseen hand as if to remind him that the living were not the only ones occupying the house.

When he told the brothers about the incident the next day, one of them scoffed and said "Thompson must have done it!" As if to remove all doubt, a light which had been clamped to an object suddenly clicked off, fell to the floor and broke. The six or seven others in the room, including the house chef, were "freaked out," as the interview goes. When their courage had returned, they examined the light. Some remembered that the lamp had never come unclamped before, and, in order to be removed, had to be physically unclamped and pulled off the object by someone.

Other feats of levitation were performed in the presence of the brothers. A full beer resting upon a silent stereo speaker, "floated out before falling" to the floor. Falling off of a roaring speaker can be explained, but witnesses confirmed that it levitated and moved forward for a moment before crashing to the floor. The same thing happened, in another room, to a large brandy snifter sitting upon a book case. Indeed, music was playing in the room, but the recording had stopped and there was some length of silence, when the several people watched as the glass snifter "fell" the two or more feet from the book case to the wooden desk so gently that it didn't even break, barely rolled, and stopped on its side, almost as if someone had carefully lowered it to the desk.

The fraternal bonds of brotherhood run deep and lasting, and a young man's allegiance to his "house" can extend well into his adulthood...and sometimes beyond.

Phi Gamma Delta—"Fiji"—is now a pleasant place to live and study...for most of the time. It is located on the southern end of the campus, not too far from the stadium, next to haunted Brua Hall[3] and just a short walk from the library. It has been the scene of a number of remarkably raucus parties over the years and for a long time was known for the annual "Fiji Island" party. The party was held in the winter and the brothers would serve drinks with little paper umbrellas and hire a local contractor to bring in enough sand to create a "beach" near the house. No matter how miserable the weather, the "uniform" for the party was shorts, shirtsleeves, and—for the very brave—swimsuits and sandals.

But one late autumn night, the place became not a house of fun and frivolity, but instead a house of fiery horror.

The newspaper clippings tell some, but not all of what may have happened. *The Gettysburg Times* screamed the headline, "College Senior Dies In Frat House Fire: Top Floor Of Phi Gam House On Campus Burns Before Dawn; 18 Escape." But there were 19 in the house.

The one victim, according to the coroner, died of "burns all over the body." The firemen who responded to the alarm said that the fire had been smoldering for over an hour before the smoke roused some of the other brothers. After they removed the young man they reported that it was possible that the student had been sitting in an overstuffed chair in which the fire may have started. He appar-

Phi Gamma Delta fraternity house, Gettysburg College

ently awakened and started for a window that opened onto a fire escape behind the building. He was agonizingly close to escaping when he collapsed. His body was found only a foot and a half from the window.

The brother who discovered the fire first smelled smoke and saw a "wall of flames" in front of the victim's room. They attempted to put out the fire with water and fire extinguishers, but were driven back by superheated air generated by the fire. The state police investigator thought the fire was started by careless smoking, but an "official source" later said that the victim had earlier set off some fire crackers in the house at about 4:30 that morning. Sparks caused by the explosions were apparently extinguished by the victim using a pillow. One can imagine the student bringing the deadly pillow back into his room and tossing it onto the chair then sitting on it and falling asleep, never knowing he carried back into his room his own fate. By 5:30 or so the sparks were smoldering, and by 6 a.m. the "wall of flame" was engulfing the room and the student.

The house was eventually cleaned up and repopulated. Though there was death and horror in the one third floor room, it too was reoccupied, and has continued to be since the fire. And yet, something is not quite right there.

There are reports that during one late-night study session that continued into the early morning hours, several brothers were present when, suddenly, the lights went out. There, standing in the far corner of the study room was a whispy form of a human....

42

No other explanation or description of the figure accompanies the notes.

And there is the recurring and frightening "nightmare" that students continue to have, which awakens them with that certain cold chill, that feeling of inescapability, as if you were trapped by whatever it is that has entered your most private slumber.

Other students are awakened from their sleep by the shout of "Fire!"—a nightmare, some say; no, say others: the cry is so loud and distinct that it must be real. These certain students are always the ones who have been assigned to the room in which that horrible, frightening cry once echoed in deadly earnest.

SLEEP ETERNAL?

Dead, but sceptered sovereigns who still rule us from the dust.
— Monument to Confederate dead at
Johnson's Island Prison in Sandusky, Ohio

We revisit the Civil War-era house on Baltimore Street, with the modern section added to it, where a young soldier seems trapped, fated to remain stuck in the older section of the house while young men of his age—but not his time—enjoy the youthful life that he was so cruelly denied. As they party, he can only watch and mourn a childhood that was snatched away from him far too soon by war.[1]

He is often seen observing the revelers from the old section of the house as the party goes on. And they sometimes see him. Those who have seen him, wave and encourage him to join them, thinking he is merely a younger brother of one of the residents. But it is never to be. He is no more a younger brother than he is alive....

It was a Sunday night. No party was raging in the house. Instead, there was sleep. The doors were locked. It was in the middle of the night, moving on to morning.

But one student was still awake, engaged in what is known to college students as "pulling an all-nighter"—staying up all night studying for an exam the next day. He was in the basement, which had been fixed up as a study area for the students. Every light was extinguished, except for the small lamp by which he was studying.

All was quiet except for that marvelous cacophony of learning going on in the student's head—though, he admitted, by this time in the morning, the roar of discovery had subsided a bit. While deep in thought, his attention was directed to a small noise above his head. Tilting an ear toward the ceiling, he heard what he thought was the upstairs door to the outside opening. He was immediately confused, because he knew everyone had gone to bed a few hours before, and he had heard no one get up and go out. As he listened to the sound, he realized that there indeed were footsteps, moving slowly, lightly from the kitchen to the front door. What impressed him the most about them is that the steps were not of anyone of adult size—no one of his housemates' sizes—but instead were of a small person, or perhaps a youngster.

For a good eight to ten minutes he listened as the steps slowly made their way from the kitchen out to the front room and back. As he stood, he heard the steps pass across the floor, just inches above his head. He could practically feel them brush his head, and the hair on the back of his neck stood.

Slowly, he made his way to the stairs, hoping that the intruder would not be dangerous. Gaining courage, he was convinced by the lightness of the footfalls that the stranger was much smaller than he. By coincidence, as the student walked through the cellar, the footsteps above his head paralleled his own as they both approached the door that stood between their very different worlds.

As he began to ascend the stairs, the student's gaze was caught by something strange: there, from beneath the door to the first floor came a luminescence, a glowing that began to stretch across the top step and light up his surroundings. He froze on the stairs as the light grew brighter and brighter until it began to pierce the cracks of the old door and reach out to caress his chest and face. The oddest thing about it, he recalled, was that the light only went halfway up the door, as if the source, whatever it might be, was small in stature.

Curiosity slowly overcame reason. The student fought a pounding heart and reached reluctantly to the doorknob to see what—or who—it was that gave off such a radiance. As he touched the doorknob, the light vanished. He found himself at the top of the stairs in complete darkness.

He opened the door and peered into the upstairs, but no one was there. He walked into the room and looked around for his housemates, but they were all still upstairs sound asleep.

An experience that can perhaps be explained by too much late-night coffee? Or by the heightened imagination perhaps brought by an over-tired mind? We can try to explain it away, but the former student will not. He knows what he experienced that night, when he stood on this side of the door to another world.

EDEN ABANDONED

...this fell sergeant, Death,
Is strict in his arrest...

—*Hamlet,* Act V, scene ii

Of primary importance in the early history of our country were taverns where travelers, weary from a long day on horseback or in a carriage, could rest, eat, and sleep before continuing their journey.

Gettysburg's location on one of the main roads from Philadelphia to Pittsburgh made it one of those stopovers containing a number of public houses scattered along what is now U.S. Route 30.

After the decisive battle, several Gettysburgians remembered a number of strangers who arrived a few weeks before the battle, drank at the local taverns, conversed with some of the locals asking questions of roads and their composition and where they led, and generally observing the amounts of cattle and horses in the vicinity. No doubt this was happening in most of the towns in southern Pennsylvania; that Gettysburg would later be the battle-site made their presence before the battle more exciting and noteworthy.

Some of them probably stopped at Frederick Herr's tavern and "publick house" on the road to Cashtown. Some may have stopped at the Eagle Hotel on the corner of Washington and Chambersburg Streets or the old Union Hotel on Chambersburg Street midway between Washington Street and the "diamond," as the town square was called.

Regardless where they stopped, they soon left with their heads full of knowledge about the nearby towns and roads. No doubt the Confederate officers used the information gathered by the "strangers" in this, their northernmost invasion of the war. Shortly, the spies were replaced by men under arms: first, Confederates under Gen. Jubal Early marching through Gettysburg on June 26, 1863; then Union cavalry clopping out the Chambersburg Road on June 30. Union infantry arrived, marching hard to relieve the cavalrymen after their fight on the morning of July 1. Finally, the Union army retreated rapidly past the old hotels on Chambersburg Street with Confederates of the Army of Northern Virginia in pursuit.

After the battle was over, no one really knows what happened in the old Union Hotel. Most likely it too became a temporary hospital for the wounded; practi-

James Gettys Hotel, Chambersburg Street

cally every other shelter in Gettysburg did. If it did, that may help explain the remarkably vivid—and remarkably frightening—experiences owners and employees of the hotel have had.

Over the years the old hotel changed hands a number of times. It was finally bought and renamed the James Gettys Hotel after one of Gettysburg's earliest settlers. In 1983 the James Gettys Hotel was being remodeled by the Crist family, relatives of the owners. They were cleaning the interior of the structure. As a rule they would leave all the interior doors propped or standing open and unlocked. But there was one seemingly self-propelled door to one room that would be closed and locked whenever they returned in the morning or after taking a break. The occurrence was written off as merely a coincidental nuisance until one particular day.

Their son was in the room cleaning up by himself, when suddenly the door to that room (and only that room) slammed shut and locked. The family had to come and get him out. Try as he might, he couldn't unlock the door and was frantically pounding on the door for someone to release him.

His mother later casually mentioned the incident to the woman who ran the American Youth Hostel next door. The Youth Hostel would rent rooms from the hotel when it was overbooked. The woman just stared at her with a look of incredulity on her face. "I had two men staying in that room," she finally said. "One was out and one was left behind. The one left behind had the same experience of the door closing by itself and locking him in. He had to crawl out the window and onto a roof to escape."

Sometime in the mid-1980s, the manager for the hotel had closed everything up for the night and had gone next door to the Blue Parrot Bistro. A friend came in and mentioned to him that he must have left the basement lights on in the hotel. The manager disagreed; he was certain he had turned all the lights off. Before he left for home, however, he decided to check anyway. Sure enough, as he peered in the door to the old hotel it looked like the basement lights were on.

He unlocked the place again and went to the cellar door. He opened the door. Emanating weirdly from the cellar was indeed a light. But oddly, as the manager checked the light switches at the top of the stairs he found that he had been right: he had turned them all off when he locked up for the night.

Not knowing what to expect, he cautiously descended the stairs to see what was causing the mysterious light. He said he was apprehensive because, as he carefully descended, he got an incredibly eerie feeling. He got down three or four steps—enough to look into the basement toward the light source, and there, standing in a vaporous cloud of light, was a lone Confederate soldier.

Frightened completely now, he yelled at the apparition, "What are you doing down here?" and "Who are you?" several times. At that, the apparition seemed take a few steps backward into a dirt-floored room, the farthest one back into the basement. The room, according to legend, had been used during the Battle of Gettysburg as a temporary hospital. The soldier backed into this room and continued to back up until he got to the farthest wall...then vanished through the back wall and into the very earth behind the hotel. With that, the vaporous light extinguished. Now in the dark, the manager rapidly found his way to the top of the stairs and out of the building.

When he told the owners what had happened, they first teased him: perhaps he had spent a little too much time at the Blue Parrot before returning to the hotel. But, in a conversation with his wife later, she assured them that her husband had been totally and truly frightened by whatever it was that he saw in the basement that night. He certainly wasn't making it up, and, for a long, long time he refused to descend into the basement for anything.

THE WOMAN IN WHITE...REVISITED

A strange and somber shadow rose up ghost-like
from the haunts of memory or habit,
and rested down over the final parting scene.
— Joshua L. Chamberlain

If indeed the original legend of "The Woman in White" at Spangler's Spring is true, then there may be more than one female spirit who wanders eternally the few hundred yards encompassed by the battlefield and the roads leading south.

The original "legend" was of a woman who had committed suicide over a broken love-pact, who now, whenever a promise is broken, strides the misty grounds of the area, never to rest until promises are no longer broken.[1]

But subsequent sightings, and the input from one of the country's most renowned psychics, have either added more information to the old legend, or indicate still another "Woman in White" who walks endlessly and forever.

Of course, there have always been the stories coming from dozens of graduating classes from Gettysburg College of the apparition seen at the Pennsylvania Monument. For years, some of the fraternities were allowed to conduct their initiation rites at midnight at the Pennsylvania Monument—appropriate in the past when the school was called Pennsylvania College; appropriate even in recent years, since the college was renamed after the town and the battlefield upon which the magnificent monument stands.[2]

Upon occasion, after the ceremonies were over and the men were preparing to leave the site, a glance back at the woods to the west or to the east of the monument would reveal a pale wraith, floating above the ground toward them, a diaphanous, white gown flowing behind her. The congratulations were cut short and the battlegrounds departed posthaste.

This author was attending a program put on by the Gettysburg Civil War Round Table. Some local historians had enlisted the aid of a psychic in a trip around the battlefield and she was explaining her feelings on, as Joshua Chamberlain called it, "this deathless field."

After the talk a man and a woman approached me, introduced themselves, and asked, since I had written about her, did I know the name of the famous "Woman in White"? I had to admit that I had no clue as to her name, but was curious enough at their question to ask, "Why?"

"Because we think she lives in our house."

My surprise was probably written on my face. They proceded to tell me how, since they bought their Civil War-era house on the Baltimore Road, they have seen at the top of their stairs a young woman walking—no, floating—along the upstairs hallway.

I made an appointment to visit with them, and when I arrived at their house, I realized that it was, as the crow flies, only a couple hundred yards from Spangler's Spring. The woman explained, as we stood out on the porch, an unusual architectural feature of having two doors almost side-by-side in the front of the house of that style of farmhouse. The one door was used daily as an entrance and exit; the other door led into what was once a formal parlor, and was used by each family member only once—when he or she was being carried out of the house in a casket. An old Pennsylvania Dutch superstition, no doubt.

Entering the house (using the *correct* door) she pointed to the stairway just to the left of the entrance. At the top of the stairway was where she had seen the ghostly woman in white. The woman described her as having long hair, wearing what seemed to her as a sort of gown. She distinctly remembered three buttons at the front. The woman's hands were indistinct, as were her facial features.

She said that almost immediately after they had moved in, her young son came down from his bedroom upstairs and asked to have his bed moved against the wall. She asked why, but the youngster refused to explain. The bed was moved and no more was said about it, until she mentioned seeing the female apparition to her family for the first time around the kitchen table. Her husband poked fun at her, as did the rest of the family, until the youngster piped up, "I saw her too! That's why I wanted my bed moved." Their laughter was silenced.

All of the family members saw her, at one time or another, in one stage of materilization or another. The husband saw her once, but an incomplete image. Their other son saw her too. But the woman has seen her at least a dozen times.

I had no explanation for her. I knew that the house had no doubt been used as a hospital; it was directly in the rear of the Union fishook line on the main road to Baltimore. So when Jim Cooke, a local radio personality asked me to set up a couple of "haunted" houses for him to broadcast from on Halloween, Joe and Collette's came immediately to mind; it would be an opportunity to bring psychic Karyol Kirkpatrick in to give her impressions of the house.

As always, we didn't tell Karyol where she was going, or any history of the house before we got there. As soon as she stepped out of the vehicle, she began talking about Native American spirits in the area. She felt the strong spirit of the hawk and the bear; she smelled the smoke from what she thought was a peace pipe; there were the spirits of slaughtered animals lingering; and graves—Native American graves—somewhere to the north of the house.

Inside the house she got the distict impression of "irons in the fire"—cauterization of bleeding arteries and veins ongoing. She felt the presence of a veterinarian who had been pressed into service to practice on people. She got the feeling of someone of French ancestry inside, and felt some bad, or "heavy" energies. Then she began picking up on the battle: there were "confronting" energies, and the image in her mind of a white flag. "This area is peaceful," she said. (At least it was relatively so, being behind the Union lines.)

In the second floor bedroom she felt both Confederate and Union soldiers: "Lots of soldiers died here." Not just dying, she said, but being killed. The damage was not intentional, but just came this way. She felt a German doctor there once, giving guidance. She said the dying were sent to the cellar so the noise wouldn't bother the others. She got the smell of dying in her nostrils.

She felt that there were religious persons who had moved in—Amish perhaps—who brought the strong energy of healing. There had been a "lot of praying to create a lighter force in order for the men there to journey to a higher level."

Descending into the cellar, she felt the remnants of six or seven people dying: she smelled again the odor of death. There once was an entranceway to the cellar, she felt, one that has since been closed off, and had been used for removing the dead.

Once upstairs again, she felt the strong presence of a priest and a nun who had come to help with the dead and dying. Suddenly Karyol got the feeling that a child was taken by scarlet fever in the northeast bedroom. The baby's name was "Gay, or Jay...Iva, or Eva Gay," who had died. Suddenly switching topics again, according to what she was allowed to see, she said it was the priest who was of French descent.

She went up into the attic while the owners and I stayed at the top of the stairs where the apparition in white had been seen so many times. The woman was surprised—in fact, seemed a little disappointed—that Karyol, after nearly forty-five minutes in the house, hadn't mentioned a thing about the woman in white. Karyol came down from the attic with her impressions.

She received the name "Garland" while up there. She thought that the attic—stifling as it might have been in July 1863—was used as the recovery room for the men who had been operated upon in the house.

Things got quiet as the owners and I looked at one another wondering whether we should say anything about the apparition in white which had appeared so many times right on the very spot where Karyol stood. Finally, the woman piped up. "This is where I have seen a woman in white, Karyol. Did you get any impression of a woman dressed in white while you were up here?"

"Oh," said Karyol, almost casually. "That's the nun."

Of course, I thought. Not all nun's habits are black; some dress in white. Could this be our woman in white, who reappears year after year, caring beyond the grave for those once placed in her tender care?

"Maria was her name," Karyol said. She felt a very good energy from her. She is, however, "not a constant presence," Karyol observed.

Of course not, I thought. She's splitting her time between here, the Pennsylvania Monument, and Spangler's Spring.

What did we witness at the Civil War house on the road to Baltimore? Historians will say that very little of what Karyol said can be documented. But how

Rocky hillock north of Spangler's Spring

much of what happened during the battle of Gettysburg has gone undocumented? Of course not every word was written down; not every name of every nun or priest or doctor or townsperson who volunteered their services was recorded. We historians are constrained to only write about what can be documented; and so much more happened here that remains undocumented. Should we claim it never happened just because no one wrote it down? Of course not. Is Karyol really tapping into undocumented history, a residual energy that remains behind as a sort of spiritual history of places? For those questions, we only have an incomplete, tattered fabric of answers. And continuing experiences with the woman in white that no one can explain....

In November 1994 I received a letter from two women who had just visited Gettysburg. They had come to town specifically on Halloween to participate in the "Ghost Tour" of Gettysburg, and then to explore the battlefield, skeptically, jokingly, in search of ghosts. Their skepticism, like so many others', would soon turn to belief; their frivolity concerning the spirit world would soon descend into abject fright.

It was about 6 p.m.—after the November darkness had descended upon the fields of battle—when they first drove to Little Round Top. There was no moon, no lights. They spent an uneventful ten minutes, then continued their drive along the battlefield road.

If they had only known what had happened along their now-peaceful route, of the horrors and ironies and savage tricks fate played upon the unlucky men and boys who had once occupied the same space they did—but at a frighteningly different time. And in all the immensity of time, past and future, the distance between those traveling through the present and those gone before was a mere blink, a tiny flicker in all the light that has shone on the earth. As if to confirm that time is at best illusory and its passing not much more than that, the women found themselves at Spangler's Spring, approaching the small parking lot there, about to get a glimpse through seam in time.

Approaching the Spring area, according to their testimony, an owl flew directly in front of the car, startling both women. Pulling into the small parking area, they turned off the car. To the left was the Spring; to the right was a small, rocky hillock, with some monuments and trees. The woman who was driving thought she had heard a loud popping sound to her left and rolled down her window.

As the woman in the passenger's seat gazed at the trees to the right, to her bewilderment, one of them seemed to be brightening. She turned her head away, blinking her eyes, figuring they were having trouble adjusting after the car lights went off. She looked back at the tree. This time the light seemed to be coming through the tree itself. She blinked again; now the light seemed to be coming around the tree, not more than fifty feet from her. Her friend was still looking in the opposite direction, and neither had spoken since hearing the popping sound. Her description from her letter is probably best:

As the light became brighter I could distinguish what appeared to be a skirt billowing around the base of the tree. I gazed part way up this light and realized I was looking at the impossible—a very bright human form. As I began to look up, my friend turned to enquire if I had heard the sound at all. I did not answer nor indicate to her what I was seeing. Suddenly she said "do you see that tree?" My only reply was "uh-huh." I then realized we were both seeing something. I turned my head forward and was more than prepared to leave the area. My friend continued to look at the light and said "oh my God, her face is so beautiful." I could not bring my self to look again. My friend then stated "this is so sad, so terribly sad," and began to cry having tears stream down her face without apparent reason. She later told me a feeling of overwhelming sadness came over her, as well as what she describes as a feeling of electrical shock or current, so much so that it caught her breath. As she continued to look the area of brightness began to move toward our vehicle and I wanted to leave....

Panic grew as a palpable presence as the whispy, brightening figure approached. The driver was virtually blinded by her tears and could not see to drive. They got the car started and the passenger, desperate now to leave, actually helped steer the car. As they began slowly to leave the area lighted by some unearthly glow, the owl passed in front of the car again. The driver's tears suddenly ceased and she said that her feelings of sadness were now gone.[3]

They debated for a while whether they should return—flipped a coin as a matter of fact, and the passenger won: they would not return that night.

Later, the passenger had the driver tell her what she saw:

My friend reports the following. To the right of the tree was a bright mist, as she watched, it rapidly coalesced and took shape. She feels she was looking at a woman with a long dress, shoulder-length hair and a heart-shaped face. She saw the dress blow around the bottom of the tree and the hair move as if blown by the wind. She did not feel any harm would have come from what we saw but did feel an emotional imbalance especially as we've already said: the sadness.

They returned to the area during daylight. Nothing they saw during the day could have explained what they saw the night before.

At a local bookstore they picked up a copy of *Ghosts of Gettysburg*, and read, for the first time, the stories of the sightings of the Woman in White at Spangler's Spring. "It was not until then," she wrote, "that we read of the 'Woman in White' or the feelings experienced by the psychic at that area. We were not aware of this until after we read it in your book. Now we are both curious. Did we actually see the 'Woman in White'? Did the emotion of sadness emanate from her? We know that we saw a bright human female form, that was not of this world."

No one knows why she remains or why she continues to bear a sadness that is so deep it affects others, drawing them helplessly into her melancholy. Only one thing is known: the legend that comes down to us from voices long stilled is less a legend now than before.

LOVE CONQUERS DEATH

I long to talk with some old lover's ghost,
Who died before the god of love was born.

—John Donne, "Love's Diety"

In this world, miracles do occur.

Though the name "Gettysburg" is linked imperishably with the three horrible days of battle in 1863 that helped determine the fate of nations—those existing then and those yet to be conceived—it has another history as well.

There are the gentle, conservative folk who have made their livings attending the farm fields and orchards, or serving the millions of visitors who make the pilgimage to Gettysburg as a sort of American *hadj*; as devout Muslims make one trip to Mecca in a lifetime, so it seems with Americans and Gettysburg.

And the people of Gettysburg over the years have lived out their lives on the outskirts or in the midst of the scene of the great conflict like so many others in other venues, in love, in pain, in jealousy, in ecstacy, in fear, inebriate, in sobriety, often in boredom and sometimes in awe. In 1918 it was in sickness and in health.

The great worldwide influenza epidemic struck Gettysburg. It hit hard at Camp Colt, the large U.S. Army tank training center where a newly graduated army officer named Dwight D. Eisenhower commanded. It was noted that the townsfolk of Gettysburg were charitable in their ministrations to the young soldiers struck down by the disease. Sadly, a number of Gettysburgians were infected as well.

One of those was Annie M. Warner. She had been married for many years to a fairly prominent and well-to-do Gettysburg businessman whose love for her was greater than any wealth he had acquired and whose faith, like some biblical parable, conquered even death.

Many Gettysburgians remember well the name of the hospital before it was changed, since it was where most were born or were made well or had loved ones pass on: Annie M. Warner Hospital on South Washington Street. The hospital was the gift John Warner promised in his prayers if the Almighty would only make his beloved Annie well again. Though near death from the influenza, she recovered, and Gettysburg got its hospital.

In Gettysburg there are some noble philanthropists, too.

The Warners lived for a time in a lovely house on Baltimore Street. The house was built in 1901 and has a formal parlor, numerous ornate rooms and a broad staircase that beckons as soon as one enters. Lately it has been an art gallery and an antique emporium, and is open to the public.

Annie Warner, as her obituary stated, was known by all for her acts of charity. Sadly, in her later years, Annie Warner's health failed. When she was 73 years old she had a bad fall, breaking one arm and badly spraining the other. Tragically, she was blind for the last four years of her life. And yet the story of the profound faith and love that John Warner had for her—literally bringing her back from the doomed—remains as a part of Gettysburg's non-battle legacy.

At one time the house was rented to college-age students. Often they would hear footsteps in the halls outside their rooms at night. At first they assumed it was one of the roommates using the facilities. But questioning one another, they discovered that none had been out of his room the entire night. They were constantly perplexed as to why their decorative posters would never adhere to the walls of their rooms. They tried everything, even tacks, but, after a while, the posters would end up on the floor. But they were really confused when framed pictures, hung on nails, would end up on the floor, below where they had been hung, not smashed, but seemingly laid there gently.

Some painting or prints would be lifted off their hooks and placed just below, reversed, with the image facing the wall.

One of the young men began to ask around about the history of the house and heard that Annie Warner had once lived there, and that, for some reason, she had particular tastes in wall hangings. Often, he was told, she would leave the walls bare when she couldn't find something to please her, rather than hang something she did not like.

A second witness to some of the events confirmed that he too heard footsteps across the hallway when no one could be seen. He watched from across the hall as one of the pictures fell off the wall to the floor. He also mentioned that when the art gallery was occupying the structure he had heard that the owners often found framed or unframed prints, which had been facing where the customers could see them, turned completely around facing the wall in the morning when they arrived for work. Obviously, since they were interested in *selling* the prints to the customers, neither the owner nor his wife would have spent their last few minutes before closing turning prints to face the wall.

This witness felt that the spirtual presence belonged to another former resident of the house who did not like any wall ornamentation whatsoever in her home.

This, of course, is hearsay. Whether it is the charitable and much beloved Mrs. Warner who returns to her house on Baltimore Street or some other devoted to interior decorating to own her tastes, is merely legend. That *someone* unseen returns to walk the halls and stairs and redecorate the walls, however, is fact.

A SHORT WALK TO THE OTHER WORLD

At the weird midnight trumpet-call they rose from their sepulchral fields as those over whom death no longer has any power. Their pulling out for the march in the ghostly mists of dawn looked like a passage in the transmigration of souls—not sent back to work out the remnant of their sins as animals, but to be lifted to the "third plane" by those three days of the underworld,—eliminating sense, incorporating soul.

—Joshua L. Chamberlain

East High Street in Gettysburg is only a block long, running from Baltimore Street to Stratton. But, for some unexplained reason, East High has a relatively large share of the numerous brushes with the supernatural that have occurred within the borough limits of Gettysburg.

For such a short street, its history is rather remarkable. On the Baltimore Street corner is the Gettysburg Presbyterian Church where Abraham Lincoln worshiped before he delivered the Gettysburg Address. President and Mrs. Eisenhower, after they retired to Gettysburg, worshipped in the church; the pew where they sat is still there.

East High Street has a slight hill in the middle of it, so, if standing at one end of the short street, you really cannot see completely to what is going on at the other end. At the other end of High Street from the Presbyterian Church is the site of the old German Reformed Church and its graveyard. The graveyard once held the body of Jennie Wade, the only civilian killed in the battle. That was her second burial: First interred in the garden behind the house where she was killed, she was removed to this cemetery; when the cemetery was removed, Jennie finally found eternal rest in the Evergreen Cemetery on Cemetery Hill.

During the battle, Confederate soldiers wandered between their main line on Middle Street and their advanced pickets along the edge of the hill where East High Street runs. One of the buildings on East High was the old jail. It still stands today, formerly the Adams County Library, currently the beautifully restored Borough Office Building. It is believed that Confederate Gen. Robert E. Lee ascended to the roof of the building at one time to observe the position of the enemy on Cemetery and Culp's Hills, both easily visible from the spot. But it seems that any residual paranormal energy remaining in the building does not necessarily come from the great commander, nor the thousands of soldiers under the ultimate stress of possibly losing their lives at any given second. Instead, at least according to those who have worked in the building, the energy comes from one held in forced incarceration for some wrongdoing perpetrated in Gettysburg before the war came.

For years while it was the Adams County Library building, the librarians would talk about "Gus," an apparently playful spirit who would move objects, turn on the water fountain to quench an eternal thirst, ride the elevator alone and, of all things, cook food in the building. At least one librarian, just before closing the building for the night, would feel an unexplainable coldness. She reported strange odors and noises when no one else was in the building. Often, employees would enter the building in the morning after it had been closed all night and would be delighted by the smell of freshly cooked food somewhere in the edifice. They could never find the source. Someone speculated that the spirit was an inmate in the prison, or perhaps the prison cook. Someone else named the busy chef "Gus." During 1950 "Gus" was so active that at the annual dinner meeting of library supporters, an extra chair was placed at the head table so that the meeting could continue without interruption.[1]

While "Gus" rules his domain inside, the general vicinity outside the building seems to be filled, at least according to some local residents, with the spirits of those seemingly trapped in the Civil War-era.

Built as the County Jail, the former Adams County Library is now the Gettysburg Borough building

A former resident of Gettysburg wrote to the author in 1994. He related an experience that happened one night in the late 1960s. He had just attended a high school dance—the high school sits just below the present borough building—and had walked up to his car parked in the library parking lot. He had gotten in his car and placed the key in the ignition when something caught his peripheral vision. There, sitting in the back seat on the passenger's side, was what appeared to be a soldier. The young man got enough of a glimpse of him to see that he was in his late teens or early twenties, wore some sort of a short jacket, "not ornate, but not ordinary," the color of tan or butternut. When he turned to fully confront the unwanted passenger, he was gone. He said that recently seeing a Civil War reenactor wearing a short, butternut jacket reminded him of the incident.

At the corner of High and Stratton Streets was the site of the old graveyard for the German Reformed Church. A young woman once related how she and a friend were walking down the street from about where the Borough Building is, to the Trinity United Church of Christ. It was between 9 and 10 p.m. It just so happened to be Halloween, for they were returning home from the Gettysburg Halloween parade. Suddenly, she saw a tall man dressed in a long black coat with tails and a stovepipe hat emerge from the solid brick wall of the United Church of Christ—which replaced the old German Reformed Church—as if it were not even there. Though there was a door nearby, he apparently didn't even need it. He "sort of floated across the street in front of us," she recalled. His face was not distinguishable, but existed only in outline form. He floated over to the house which now stands on the corner, and then drifted to the area where the old cemetery used to be. At first she thought he was an undertaker. But once he reached the site of the old cemetery, he disappeared, absorbed by the earth as if returning to his permanent resting place. But when he vanished at the former site of the cemetery, she and her friend didn't stay around long enough to observe more—they ran for home.[2]

Upon particular—and peculiar—occasions we are waking dreamers, one and all, following our future, all walking slowly toward Death as Death walks quickly toward us. For aren't we all merely ghosts in waiting?

STONE SHADOWS

Knowledge by suffering entereth,
And life is perfected by death.
— Elizabeth Barrett Browning

We turn again to Gettysburg College, once called Pennsylvania College, made notorious by the great carnage around its hallowed halls. A tiny school then, its few buildings filled almost immediately with the helpless wounded. They suffered under the surgeon's heartless saw, languished for a few days, suffered more, and then, often as not, passed on. They were taken outside to the once-manicured grounds of the college, and buried, without tender words, without grieving family, and without holy ceremony.

While the Union soldiers were exhumed in the few months after the battle, Confederates awaited in their uneasy graves until the first years of the 1870s, then were unearthed and packaged—what was left of them—in boxes and shipped to several railroad stations in the South, there to be picked up, transported and buried for the most part *en masse*.

"Did they get all of them?" is the macabre question everyone thinks and a few even ask. The answer: No, probably not. And what they "got" was certainly not much: Tattered bits of muddy cloth, chewed by insects for its sweat and blood; skulls and soil-clogged teeth, the brotherly grins or fatherly smiles sloughed away into the loam below now; large bones of the arm and leg, the muscles made hard by months of marching and carrying the heavy musket gone, reabsorbed into Mother Earth—*ashes to ashes and dust to dust.* What once constituted the noble sons and brothers and fathers of the South was mostly left forever in this one corner of hated Yankeedom. It would have galled them, if they only knew....

As the college expanded over the years, buildings rose over some of the erstwhile graveyards, the bits and pieces of butternut cloth (and the far more valuable bits of men) were displaced again and again by the shovel and later the backhoe. The buildings became modern and numerous, the grounds manicured again. One can almost forget, strolling across the lovely green campus, what a hideous mulch once fertilized the lush green below.

We return to Stevens Hall, apparent home of the Blue Boy, who hovers outside a third floor window on certain cold nights and is seen peering in at the warm students within.[1] One room on the third floor seems particularly susceptible to the earthly wanderings of unearthly creatures.

Sometime in 1977, a woman living in this particular room was alone one night. Her eye was drawn to the corner of the room where, suddenly, out of nothingness, appeared a young man. According to her interview, he was "semi-transparent," seemed to her to be in his "early 20s," and radiated a light of some sort. The transparency evidently affected his ghostly clothing as well, for she could not identify the historical period of his attire. As weirdly as he materialized, so did he dematerialize.

Same room, two years later in the month of October: a different woman was also alone in the room. The door was locked. Suddenly, as if propelled by some powerful force, the locked door flew open. Later she mentioned this strange experience to two of her roommates. To her surprise they both confirmed that in the past month or two, the same thing had happened to them as well.

A month later, just before the Thanksgiving break, the first woman was standing in her room facing her stereo system when she felt something—a presence, she described it—staring at her back. As she swung around quickly to see who had entered her room, her arms passed through an incredibly cold spot hanging in the air. No one was in the room with her.

At a later time, another of the roommates felt the same weird presence, the same staring from behind, with no one else in the room.

View on North Washington Street

Finally, one evening, the women had all retired for the night, but none was yet asleep. Suddenly, a light shot across the room from the door to the window. Two of the roommates saw it. Both agreed that it came from the door and not the window where a light from outside should have emanated. Both agreed that it was something inside the room. As they all lay there wondering what the strange, darting light was, they were startled by the loud sound of something falling to the floor from the table upon which the stereo was placed. Jumping from bed, one of them flipped on the light, and to their amazement, absolutely nothing was on the floor next to the table. The noise itself was a phantom.[2]

Why would Gettysburg College have so much psychic activity? If one believes in the theory that poltergeists, or "noisy ghosts," are actually caused by psychokinesis, or mental energy that is somehow transformed into physical energy, then the explanation is simple: the young men and women who inhabit the college merely have a great deal of energy, and some of it is manifested through psychokinesis.

But just as plausible is the theory that, because of the college's location on what was once the battlefield (and a graveyard), a multitude of paranormal activities would happen there anyway. Because so many students are there on the site, they have more of a chance of being "in the right place at the right time," to witness the activity. One must wonder, if this is the case, what happens out on the darkened battlefields after the National Military Park is closed down for the night and the rangers are home safe in bed. A spirits' holiday, perhaps?

A house on North Washington Street now belonging to the college is named in its official historical records as the Robert Tate house and dates back to 1858. Tax records suggest that the house remained virtually unaltered until 1892, and was altered periodically several times after that. Robert Tate, the original owner, was a harnessmaker. His house, being near Old Dorm on the Pennsylvania College campus, was one of the first in the rear of the Union lines on July 1, 1863. Then, as the Federals were driven back in the afternoon, the Tates' home was in the rear of the Confederate lines. Since Old Dorm was used as a hospital (and since there was a superabundance of wounded after the first day's fighting), it is also likely that the Tates' gentle home, as well as others on North Washington Street, became makeshift hospitals.

And with the large numbers of wounded came the surgeons and the orderlies, walking from patient to helpless patient, from those who recently had been relieved of their limbs, to those about to be. In and out of the door they came and went, up and down the stairs from the operating rooms to the recovery rooms. It seems though, that even with the retreat of their armies, some of the surgeons and their helpers haven't themselves completely left....

The house is now used as a resource center for Gettysburg College, and some of the students who sign up to work there...won't. It's the footsteps, they say. The constant walking that won't cease. No, they don't get paid enough to listen to that at night!

Even the administrators who work there have their unexplainable tales. One dean working late at night suddenly heard a number of people coming down the stairs. He was shocked, since he thought he had been alone in the structure when he had returned an hour before to work a few extra hours. It seems he was right. As he turned to confront the crowd apparently descending noisily down the stairs, the sounds suddenly quieted, and he saw no one on the stairs.

But after dark are not the only hours when the invisible intruders arrive. One administrator remembers coming in early for work one morning in the autumn of 1990. Since they weren't officially open, she locked the door behind her. As she settled at her desk on the first floor, she heard movements and walking upstairs. She didn't go upstairs at first and just assumed that the dean had arrived at work even earlier than she.

Some time passed. She had some business upstairs and ascended to the second floor. Expecting to say good morning to the dean, she was perplexed when she realized that no one was on the second floor. As she stood there, she distinctly heard the downstairs door—which she had still not unlocked—open and then shut as if someone was leaving.

She went downstairs, and, of course, there was no one there, and no one outside the door. Finally, at 9:30 a.m., the dean arrived at the office, and took his first steps through the door that day. Who then, she wondered—and still to this day wonders—was the mysterious presence wandering the house just a few feet above her head? Some conscientious surgeons, perhaps, returning to check on patients long dead; surgeons who have finally learned that all their efforts at saving the men were in vain, since Death invariably makes the final scalpel cut of all.

ARABESQUES UPON WATER

I am become Death, the shatterer of worlds.
—Bhagavad Gita

A little over a mile west of Gettysburg is where it all started. Confederate infantry advancing from Cashtown bumped into Union cavalry on a ridge. It was just a few, well-spaced, dismounted horsemen and some stretched-out footsoldiers popping away at each other. But it would escalate and turn the land around Gettysburg into fields of death that have become ghost-gardens where long-gone spirits bloom unbidden.

Frederick Herr ran his brick tavern and "publick house" for travelers along the Cashtown-to-Gettysburg road. His family had owned the land for so long that the ridge upon which the tavern stood was known as "Herr's Ridge." For years, early "tourists" and businessmen, weary from their travels, found rest and solace by the small corner bar in the front room and in a game of chance elsewhere in the building.

The building was built in 1815, the same year Napoleon fought at Waterloo. One Thomas Sweeney owned the building first. It was called the Sweeney Stand. In 1827 Sweeney went bankrupt and in 1828 Frederick Herr bought it, improved it, and held it until he died in 1868.

Numerous tales have come and gone of the old building and its inhabitants and owners. Frederick Herr made his own whiskey. One of the occupants of the building was known for his ability to counterfeit money on a press in the basement of the old structure. There was David Lewis, a.k.a. "Lewis the Robber," who frequented the old tavern and was subsequently hanged in the 1840s for some misadventures no doubt associated with his nickname. There are stories of the upstairs being used, at one time, as a brothel.

But for the years the old tavern served passers-by with food, drink and overnight shelter, life was calm on the pastoral ridge just west of the tiny crossroads town that could be seen in the distance. Then Hell made a house call.

Sometimes it seems that certain places have been marked by fate for renown. This of course, can be seen perfectly in retrospect. But the collision of two great armies outside of Gettysburg was an accident. Neither commander wanted to fight here; neither pointed to Gettysburg—nor to Mr. Herr's tavern—and said, "Here's where the greatest battle of the war will be fought." Once the battle was joined, however, the two armies began the slaughter with a hideous will. No one ever thought that the battle begun around Frederick Herr's brick tavern would itself become a Waterloo.

Vedettes of the Federal cavalry under Brig. Gen. John Buford encamped the night of June 30, 1863, along Herr's Ridge. The next morning they were pushed back as Maj. Gen. Henry Heth's Confederate infantry advanced from Cashtown. From Herr's Ridge, Heth launched attacks upon the cavalry, and then upon the Union infantry of Maj. Gen. John Reynolds who replaced them. Artillery shells from near-sighted Willie Pegram's Confederate guns whizzed over and past the old tavern, and Lt. John Calef's Federal guns replied, sending their shells to explode near the ancient brick walls. One exploded in a corner of a second floor room. Where weary travelers once lay down to rest for the next day's journey, dying soldiers collapsed in heaps to rest for their journey to the next world.

All day the killing and dying went on as Confederates attacked from west of the tavern and barn—then from the north and finally the east—toward the Union lines closer to Gettysburg. Robert E. Lee rode past Frederick Herr's tavern, as did generals A. P. Hill and James Longstreet and dozens of other high and low ranking officers. It was probably just beyond the tavern, a little closer to Seminary Ridge, where Lee realized that his men were winning the battle at that point, and so made his decision to continue the action, making the name "Gettysburg" as famous and imperishable as his own.

After the fighting died down, the tavern and barn filled rapidly with the cast-offs of battle, and the surgeons came with their scalpels and saws, and the gravediggers closely following in the pale footsteps of the grim scythe-wielder, Death.[1] The 33rd Virginia, as well as the 11th and 26th North Carolina Infantry regiments, left half a dozen men buried in the hated Yankee clay around Frederick Herr's tavern. □ A traveler to the tavern shortly after the battle wrote that he thought a company of soldiers were "put up" after the battle in the tavern. He and his companions used the water in the well of the tavern, but after a while they began to get sick, and the water began to smell. Thinking there were dead frogs in it, they pumped it out: "By and by here comes up a little piece of wrist and thumb...."[2]

Frederick Herr's tavern was eventually sold and became the Reynolds Hotel, then, by 1910, a school of music operated by Maude Bucher. Later it was private housing. Finally, in the tavern's long and storied history it was purchased by Steve Wolf, who began the laborious task of restoring the building to its original look and use as a "tavern-stand and publick house."

True to the pattern of increased paranormal activities during a restoration, strange, unexplainable events began to occur. One of the restorers, as she began removing wallpaper in the old tavern, began to feel what she described as a distinctly unfriendly presence. Once, as she was working alone along the stairs, she felt a rough shove, as if someone unseen were trying to push her down the stairs. Frightened, and a bit angry, she unconsciously shouted—to no one—"I'm just trying to turn it back into a tavern again!" After that confrontation with the invis-

The Herr Tavern as it appeared in 1882

ible entity, she said she felt accepted. Other than a few more "feelings," she never had another threatening event.

One day Steve, the owner, and another fellow were standing at opposite ends of the bar. No one was in the bar at the time, but both men looked to the center of the empty bar, for they distinctly heard someone ask for a beer. The puzzlement displayed on their faces convinced both men that they had each heard the thirsty spirit of a tavern customer apparently long since departed.

Once, as they were relating this weird story, a disbelieving patron ridiculed them. His laughter was abruptly halted, however, when he felt what he swore was a hand on his shoulder pushing him off the stool where he sat.

Unexplainable activities at the tavern are fairly commonplace. They have been reported by both employees and patrons of the bed and breakfast. Much of the activity centers around the two front rooms.

A family of three was sleeping in Room 1. The woman was sound asleep; her son was sleeping on a cot right next to her. She was awakened by someone grabbing her hand and shaking it. Thinking it was her son, she turned immediately to him, but he was sound asleep, facing away from her toward the wall. She slept uneasily the rest of the night with her arms crossed tightly over her chest.

The light at the top of the stairs on the second floor has been seen flicking on, then off. Occasionally, the employees will turn off lights as they exit the building for the night; looking back, they see some of the lights still burning and must reenter the tavern—some of them reluctantly—to extinguish the lights once again.

Much of the activity reported is audible: chairs are heard moving around in adjacent rooms, sometimes sounding as if they are being thrown about. One patron of the bed and breakfast asked one morning who had been moving furniture in the attic in the middle of the night. Of course, no one had, and when the manager was requested to inspect the garret, nothing had been touched.

One of the most violent times of activity was when two women were doing a photo shoot on ghosts for a tabloid newspaper. Apparently, there wasn't enough psychic activity for them and they "spiced" things up; when the article finally appeared, it had some fabrications. On the morning they were to check out, some of the employees thought they were having a fight in Room 1: it sounded as if they were throwing furniture at each other. The employees checked the guest register. The pair had checked out hours before. The manager and employees ascended to the room. When they opened the door, in spite of the tremendous racket, everything remained untouched, exactly where it had been placed when last inspected.

At breakfast one morning, one of the guests asked if the tavern does door checks, having heard her doorknob rattle in the middle of the night. One after another the other guests in the dining room piped up and said, yes, they had heard their doorknob rattle, all at about 3 a.m. Needless to say, no one at the tavern checks doors at 3 in the morning; no *living* being employed there, anyway.

The manager's first experience with whomever it is that stalks through the tavern was on a Sunday morning. No one was checked into the bed and breakfast at the time, about 10:30 in the morning. From upstairs came the heavy pounding of boots on the floor. Her first thought was that someone had come quietly in the door while she had been distracted. She bravely "armed" herself with the closest thing she could find—a heavy water pitcher—and ascended the stairs to confront the intruder. Expecting to see a large, booted man around any corner, she cautiously, systematically checked everywhere: in every room, behind every door, behind every shower curtain, and found not a soul. She returned to her work downstairs, worked for twenty minutes, and had nearly convinced herself in that time that she must have imagined the relentless stomping. Suddenly, from upstairs, came the heavy sound of a booted man walking. She distinctly heard him walk, then pause, then walk some more, then pause again. Finally, the restless, rogue entity ceased its walking.

Doors already locked are heard to close and lock again: a couple in Room 4 one evening thought someone had walked in on them in the middle of the night. When they jumped out of bed to face the intruder, no one was there and the door remained locked. At another time, the manager and her husband were stranded at the tavern by a heavy snowstorm. They decided to make the best of it and ensconced themselves for the night in Room 5. At 1 a.m. they were awakened when they heard the locked door to Room 5 close and lock again. The husband was certain that the door had been locked when they had ascended, and so the sound was puzzling. He checked the door again to ensure it was indeed locked. Then, at 9 a.m., the stranded couple heard the locked door below them open and close, and heard the distinctive sound of the latch falling in place. It was as if, 130 years after his death, an unseen innkeeper was still securing his property.

Doors locked after business hours, when checked one last time, will be found unlocked, as if someone, somewhere, were expecting a late arriving guest.

One night a woman staying in Room 3 was angry. "I thought you didn't allow children here," she complained to the management. "Someone has a baby in Room 4." She had heard a baby crying and a woman singing softly to it to sooth it. She distinctly heard the woman and the baby walk past her door and into Room 4. At that moment the man in Room 4 emerged. He and his wife had no child in their room and even invited them in to check. And the manager assured the woman that no one with a baby had checked in to the bed and breakfast.

Previous research, however, seems to have indicated that Frederick and Susan Herr had tragically lost a beloved baby to some childhood illness.

The manager was working away from the bar area late one night after everything was closed up. She heard the bar door open and close and the water turn on. Thinking it was the owner coming in for a late snack, she decided to play a practical joke and scare her boss. She took off her shoes to sneak up on him. When she got to the bar, she flipped on the light, but no one was at the sink; the water was off; all the doors were closed and locked. Her little prank backfired. The only one she managed to frighten was herself.

It is indeed a distinctive, unmistakable sound of water running in the stainless steel sink. A waitress has heard it so many times while alone in the tavern that she ignores it by now, realizing that when she checks it, she will, as in all the times past, find no water running. It's as if to quench some invisible thirst, invisible water runs.

The kitchen seems to retain a lot of unexplainable activity. The pastry chef said she once heard what sounded like an entire metal tray of dishes being dropped and shattered, but inspection around the kitchen indicated that not a thing had fallen. Later she heard the sound of pots and pans being dropped into the sink. When she went to the sink, she found no pots and pans there.

Modern machines and conveniences are affected, as if someone who cares about the old building is experimenting with them to make sure they are not harmful to the place. One night the electric credit card machine began spewing several inches of tape all on its own. Televisions have come on by themselves in Rooms 1 and 4 in the middle of the night, awakening the guests. Heaters have been turned on and telephones, which are nightly turned off to incoming calls, ring or have message lights burning when no message exists.

Most of the people who have worked in the tavern and have experienced some of the entity activity agree that there are both male and female presences: at least two and possibly three entities.

They seem to be friendly—even intimate—with the employees, for a number of them have heard their own names called out. One waitress heard someone calling her name from upstairs. Answering to the beckoning, she went upstairs to find no one, guests or employees, on that floor. Another waitress heard her name called from upstairs. It sounded, she said, as if someone was calling her name through a long tunnel. It sounded so weird, in fact, that instead of finding the source upstairs, she ran from the building.

The dishwasher came out of the kitchen to confront the manager one night. "What?" he asked, having heard his name called and assuming it was the manager who wanted him. She, however, hadn't called him. Two more times he emerged from the kitchen, growing more agitated each time, as each time he was told the same thing: no one—at least on this side of reality—had called him. Apparently, the name-calling continued: the manager said she never saw him wash dishes so fast.

The sightings people have had in Herr Tavern seem to confirm the dual entities' presence. The manager says that often you'll see something out of the corner of your eye. When you turn to focus, it goes away.

A young man was sitting in the bar waiting for his mother to come by and pick him up. He saw perfectly a man approach the door as if about to enter, then abruptly disappear. He mentioned this to one of the waitresses on duty that night, and for a while she dismissed it as a combination of a real customer who had changed his mind about entering and the over-active imagination of a youngster. That was until later that same night.

She was in the kitchen and happened to look out the open sliding doors. There, standing at the end of the bar, was a very large, tall, hulking figure. Thinking she needed to go out and explain that the bar was closed, she took her eyes off him for a fraction of a second, immediately went through the door and found that he had vanished. He could not have crossed the floor to the door in the short amount of time it took her to walk through the door into the bar. The man, his identity, and even his very existence, remain unknown and unexplained.

When cleaning the rooms by herself, the manager has heard the gentle sound of a lady's demure cough.

And finally, within the last few months, a man in Room 2, looked across the hall one night into Room 1. Standing in the room he observed what he described as a petite, blond woman. He thought she was a guest. He said hello, but she ignored him and walked toward the bed in Room 1 moving so as to be out of his line of sight. Not wanting to intrude upon another guest who obviously wanted privacy, he did not pursue the matter. He mentioned it to the management the next morning and was utterly surprised to hear that no one had been checked into that room. Believing that he may have gotten a rare glimpse into the other world, he remained awake and curious all the next night—much to the dismay of his poor wife—hoping to see the lovely blond woman again. It seems that as fickle as people can be in this life, they can apparently be just as fickle in the next. He never saw her again.

In each of the guest rooms in the Herr Tavern is a diary for the patrons to record their comments and experiences. The entries rave about the friendly employees and management, the peaceful surroundings and accommodations and the wonderful food at the tavern. Words expressing heartfelt pain at the realization of the horror of boys doing battle and dying right outside their windows are also read in the diaries. As well as the glowing comments and serious thoughts are some unusual comments relating some of the guests' unexplainable experiences. The written comments and statements during breakfast have forced the employees to name the ghosts "Fred" and "Susan" after the Herrs. Some of the guests comments follow.

1/2/93: ...the TV was suddenly turned off and not by either one of us. ...So the hospitality at the Herr's Tavern extends beyond the explicable....

11/14/93: ...(We heard the ghost)....

4/24/94: As for Fred, I think he was restless our first night here but last night he must have been elsewhere.

7/17/94: Dear Fred—You can "rest easy" knowing that your tavern is in good hands. ...Sorry you missed my [birthday] party, Fred. Or was that you tugging at my pillow last night?

7/20/94: We were told about "Fred" the ghost and I didn't think he visited us until I found my shoes laced together this morning!

8/12/94: We had a late night visit from Fred. He shook my hand (waking me up) to welcome our family to his home....

8/25-8/94: P.S. Bye Fred...Hope to see or hear you more next time.

11/27/94: ...Fred turned up in our room last night. He turned the heater on for us about 2 a.m. Thanks, Fred. We were getting cold.

12/9-10/94: Fred...rattled the fan at night & caused the phone to blink with a message when there was none.

12/29-30/94: By the way, I think Fred did introduce himself last night...thank Fred for watching over us last night.

1/1/95: (Who does the door check at 3 a.m.?)

1/29/95: The fireplace turned off around 3 a.m. Was that Fred?

2/5/95: A few strange things happened, the phone rang at 11:20, answered and no one was there, then it rang again at 3:20 a.m., none of us would get up to answer. The door at the barn opened several times, no one there, and our bedroom door kept opening....

6/12/95: Fred did come & screwed up the phones.

7/30/95: No creaking floors or knocks on the door, however, I swear I heard a lady singing light opera at 12:30 p.m. ...I turned on the television on the music channel and it all disappeared.

8/14/95: Fred's only appearance was via the telephone. We came in and the message light was on. When I picked up the phone I was connected to a Friendship Inn. The phone lights seem to respond to conversation....

Is the spirit the employees intuitively refer to as "Fred" really the former Civil War-era owner of the tavern, watching over the place and sending messages to his modern guests? With all the people—weary, thirsty travelers and caring owners, soldiers and officers, wounded and dying, and families—who have passed through the doors and stayed within the brick walls of the old tavern since 1815, it would be difficult to tell.

But notes found in Dr. Charles Emmons' files dated 1981 seem to confirm that regardless of the decade or the observers, some things continue to occur:

"In the pool room area: chairs had been knocked down off tables with a clatter. Out of corner of his eye once he thought he saw dark shadow form of a man where old bar area was. Coming down stairs he went thru cold area (and once felt cold alternately on front & back depending on which part of his body was facing a spot). Thought that was a female. ...[He] has seen nothing in Tavern but thinks there are one male & one female."

NOTES

The Premature Burial

1. Mason, W. Roy, "Notes of a Confederate Staff-Officer," *Battles and Leaders*, 3:101. Mason was appalled after the Battle of Fredericksburg at the "burial" of some of the Union dead: "But the most sickening sight of all was when they threw the dead, some four or five hundred in number, into Wallace's empty ice house, where they were found—a hecatomb of skeletons—after the war."

Tourist Season in the Other World

1. Veil, Charles Henry, *Memoirs*, Herman J. Viola, ed. (New York: Orion Books, 1993), 29-30.

Actors or Reenactors

1. Johnson, Eric, correspondence and telephone conversations, October-November, 1992.
2. Chamberlain, Joshua Lawrence, *The Passing of the Armies: An Account of the Final Campaign of the Army of the Potomac Based Upon Personal Reminiscences of the Fifth Army Corps* (New York: G. B. Putnam's Sons, 1915), 312-13.
3. Stewart, George R. *Pickett's Charge: A Microhistory of the Final Attack at Gettysburg, July 3, 1863*, (Cambridge: Houghton Mifflin Company, 1959), 141. See also Tucker, Glenn. *High Tide at Gettysburg: The Campaign in Pennsylvania*, (New York: The Bobbs-Merrill Company, Inc., 1958), 353.
4. Stewart, 157, 167.

Alone in Hell

1. McLaughlin, Jack, *Gettysburg: The Long Encampment*, (New York: Appleton-Century, 1963), 188-9.
2. Alexander, John, *Ghosts: Washington's Most Famous Ghost Stories* (Washington, D.C.: Washingtonian Books, 1975), 59-65.

Hell is for Children, Too

1. See Mark Nesbitt, *Ghosts of Gettysburg* (Gettysburg: Thomas Publications, 1991), 32.
2. The full history of the orphanage can be read in Mary Ruth Collins and Cindy A. Stouffer, *One Soldier's Legacy: The National Homestead at Gettysburg* (Gettysburg: Thomas Publications, 1993).

Brotherhood Forever
1. See "Off-off Broadway," Nesbitt, *More Ghosts of Gettysburg* (Gettysburg: Thomas Publications, 1992), 54-5.
2. Christ, Elwood W., unpublished research files of historic houses done for the Gettysburg Historic Building Survey Committee (Gettysburg: Preservation Office, Gettysburg Borough Office Building, no date).
3. See "The Play's the Thing," Nesbitt, *Ghosts of Gettysburg*, 33.

Sleep Eternal?
1. See Nesbitt, *Ghosts of Gettysburg*, 45-6.

The Woman in White...Revisited
1. See "Black Sunset," Nesbitt, *Ghosts of Gettysburg*, 68.
2. To hold initiation ceremonies on the battlefield, organizations need special permission from the National Park Service. Almost all of the roads along the battlelines are closed after 10 p.m.
3. The addition of the owl to the story is interesting. It is an element that is not needed to add to or complete the story. Often individuals relating their unexplainable experiences to me will include non-sequiters, things that have nothing to do with the story, but obviously happened at the time. These oddities, to me, mean that the person is not making up the story. No one who is making up a story would insert something that doesn't make sense.

A Short Walk to the Other World
1. Murray, Dorothy Speicher, *A Library for Adams County* (Gettysburg: Friends of the Library, 1988), 7-8.
2. Baker, Beth, "Gettysburg's Ghosts Rise on Occasion," *The Gettysburg Times*.

Stone Shadows
1. See Nesbitt, *Ghosts of Gettysburg*, 76.
2. Hettler, Kurt W., "Weird Hauntings at Gettysburg College," an unpublished paper done for Dr. Charles Emmons, submitted January 24, 1980.

Arabesques Upon Water
1. Coco, Gregory A., *A Vast Sea of Misery: A History and Guide to the Union and Confederate Field Hospitals at Gettysburg, July 1-November 20, 1863* (Thomas Publications, 1988). Coco writes that no documented evidence exists to prove the tavern and barn were field hospitals, but included the fact that bloodstains could be seen on the upstairs floor as late as 1986. He also pointed out that several surrounding sites were "possible" hospital locations.
2. Coco, 134-5.

We died, those bitter winters, believing in a spring.
When all the buds would blossom, and all the bells should ring,
Not for our own doomed selves, but for all tribes of sons unborn—
For us to plough the heavy fields, for them to reap the corn:
We died, unhalting, killed and died, that wars at last should cease,
And man, to fuller stature grow, honor us dead with Peace.

—Howard I. Chidley

Gatehouse to the Evergreen Cemetery

Mark Nesbitt was born in Lorain, Ohio. He graduated from Baldwin-Wallace College, Berea, Ohio, with a BA in English Literature. He worked for the National Park Service as a Ranger Historian for 5 years and started his own freelance writing and research business in 1977.

He is the author of *Ghosts of Gettysburg* (1991), *More Ghosts of Gettysburg* (1992), and seven other books and publications.

THOMAS PUBLICATIONS publishes books about the American Colonial era, the Revolutionary War, the Civil War, and other important topics. For a complete list of titles, please visit our website:

www.thomaspublications.com

Or write to:

THOMAS PUBLICATIONS
P.O. Box 3031
Gettysburg, PA 17325